**Barriers to Establishing Urban Ombudsmen:**
**The Case of Newark**

# INSTITUTE OF GOVERNMENTAL STUDIES

Eugene C. Lee, *Director*

The Institute of Governmental Studies was established in 1919 as the Bureau of Public Administration, and given its present name in 1962. One of the oldest organized research units in the University of California, the Institute conducts extensive and varied research and service programs in public policy, politics, urban-metropolitan problems and public administration.

A prime resource in these endeavors is the Institute's Library, comprising more than 350,000 documents, pamphlets and periodicals related to government and public affairs. The Library serves faculty and staff members, students, public officials and interested citizens.

In addition to its traditional Library holdings, the Institute administers the State Data Program, a teaching and research collection comprising a wide variety of machine-readable data dealing with state politics, policies and institutions. It includes public opinion polls, legislative roll calls, registration and voting statistics, characteristics of state legislatures and output measures of state policies and programs.

The Institute's professional staff is composed of faculty members who hold joint Institute and departmental appointments, research specialists, librarians and graduate students from a variety of social science disciplines. In addition, the Institute is host to visiting scholars from other parts of the United States and many foreign nations.

The Institute publishes books, monographs, periodicals, reprints, reports and bibliographies for a nationwide readership. The publications are intended to stimulate research, thought and action by scholars and public officials, with respect to significant governmental and social issues.

INSTITUTE OF GOVERNMENTAL STUDIES
University of California, Berkeley

# Barriers to Establishing Urban Ombudsmen: The Case of Newark

WILLIAM B. GWYN
Department of Political Science
Tulane University

1974

A publication of the Institute's Ombudsman Activities Project.
The research was funded by U.S. Office of Economic Opportunity Grant
Number CG-9041.

LIBRARY OF CONGRESS CATALOGING IN PUBLICATION DATA

Gwyn, William B
  Barriers to establishing urban ombudsmen.

  "A publication of the Institute's Ombudsman Activi-
ties Project."
  1. Ombudsman--Newark, N. J.  2.  Newark, N. J.--
Politics and government.  I.  California.  University.
Institute of Governmental Studies.  II.  Title.
JS1242.4.A4  1974      352'.0029'0973      74-11446
ISBN 0-87772-200-5

$4.50

To Norman Abrams, public servant,

for his great kindness and remarkable patience

in responding to my continual enquiries about

the Newark Ombudsman and the mysteries of

Newark politics.

# CONTENTS

# FOREWORD

We can learn from success stories, and we can also learn from thoughtful investigation of ambitious
projects that fail. As William Gwyn's title indicates
this volume is unique among the Ombudsman books published by the Institute of Governmental Studies. Some
Ombudsman offices discussed in the monographs are in
operation and have been functioning for some time;
some proposals remain only in the discussion stage; at
least one was allowed to lapse after a subsidized demonstration period. In contrast the Newark Ombudsman
came close to being established, but faltered at the
point where the city council was to name the Ombudsman.
Gwyn narrates this dramatic story, and with a thoughtful analysis of what happened, helps us understand why
events developed as they did. Moreover, he suggests
the lessons others can learn from Newark's failure to
implement the proposal.

This succinct and penetrating study is one of the
last produced by the Ombudsman Activities Project,
which was sponsored by the Institute of Governmental
Studies and financed by the Office of Economic Opportunity. Stanley V. Anderson of the Political Science
faculty at the University of California, Santa Barbara,
was the project director, and many of the studies were
conducted by faculty members associated with that campus.

The Institute is pleased to include this book in the Ombudsman series, as well as to thank the participants in the Ombudsman studies for the usefulness of their contributions and the quality of their work. Thanks are also due to Catherine Winter who did the final typing for this monograph.

Stanley Scott
Assistant Director

# PREFACE

This monograph is a revised version of a report I submitted to the Ombudsman Activities Project in the summer of 1973, as part of the project's services for the Office of Economic Opportunity. I had joined the project in June 1972 and was assigned the responsibility for assisting the Newark Ombudsman and then analyzing and assessing the operation of the office after it was established. When, however, the Newark Ombudsman failed to go into operation, it was agreed that it would be profitable to OEO and other Ombudsman advocates for me to undertake an explanation of the failure. It was hoped that such an explanation would provide information that could improve chances of establishing Ombudsmen elsewhere in the United States. Along with this major objective, my research also sought to explain how an Ombudsman came to be proposed for Newark and why the office took on the particular form it did in the ordinance. In pursuing both of these aims I inevitably accomplished a third, for the monograph is also a case study in joint federal-urban policy-making.

In revising the report for publication, I have had the great advantage of advice and additional information from several people who have read the original text: Mr. Norman Abrams of Mayor Gibson's office, Professor Stanley B. Winters of the history faculty of the Newark College of Engineering, and Professors Stanley V. Anderson, John E. Moore and Alan J. Wyner of the

Department of Political Science, the University of California, Santa Barbara.  I should like heartily to thank these men and others who have generously taken time from their busy lives to assist me, while also absolving them from any mistakes of fact or interpretation the reader may encounter.  For these, alas, the author is solely responsible.

William B. Gwyn
Tulane University
May, 1974

# I

## Evolution of the Newark
## Ombudsman Proposal

### PROPOSALS FOR A CIVILIAN REVIEW BOARD

An Ombudsman was first proposed for Newark in the wake of the July 1967 riots. For some years before the riots relations between the city's ever expanding Black population and the predominantly white police force had worsened. In 1965 CORE led a demonstration in Newark supporting the establishment of a civilian review board. This action provoked the city's Policemen's Benevolent Association (PBA), the major police union of the city, to oppose the demand by picketing City Hall.[1] The proposal came to nothing.

Following the 1967 riots, Governor Richard J. Hughes created a Select Commission to determine the causes of and remedies for civil disorders in New Jersey. Concluding that Newark's Black community had no effective means for redressing grievances against the police, the commission recommended in its report the establishment of a civilian review board.[2] Apparently expecting some reluctance on the part of Mayor Addonizio, the commission added that if the Mayor failed to act on the recommendation, legislation should be passed to allow the State Supreme Court to appoint such a board. The report placed Addonizio in a political dilemma. Not to comply with the commission's recommendation might lead to the board's being imposed on Newark by the Supreme Court, and even if that eventuality were blocked in the state legislature, failure to comply would almost certainly increase the Mayor's problems

1

with the city's Black leaders. On the other hand, the Mayor knew that the Newark police and probably many of his white supporters would be outraged if he created a civilian review board.

## THE OMBUDSMAN AS ALTERNATIVE

On February 29, 1968, Addonizio sought to dodge both horns of the dilemma by rejecting the commission's recommendation but ordering his Corporation Council Norman Schiff to make a preliminary study of the feasibility of an Ombudsman to protect the citizens of Newark against the abuse of governmental power.[3] The announcement did not go unobserved in Washington where Gersen Green, director of OEO's division of research and pilot programs, announced, "I would run a project in Newark, but it's got to be a good one." He wanted a "real Ombudsman plan" including power to subpoena witnesses and evidence.[4] Schiff's report of April 27th did indeed provide a real Ombudsman plan and the Mayor, when giving it his endorsement, stated that he anticipated OEO funds to finance the new organization.

## The Addonizio-Schiff Plan

Although no sources are mentioned in the text of the report, Schiff appears to have drawn heavily on scholarly research for background and argument and on Professor Walter Gellhorn's Model Ombudsman Statute for the actual plan.[5] The draft bill was to be introduced into the state legislature, which would establish by statute an Ombudsman in every municipality with a population over 100,000. Unable to decide on the best method of appointment, Schiff mentioned two possibilities: (1) by the Chief Justice of the New Jersey Supreme Court, and (2) by the Mayor with the approval of the governing body. However appointed, the Ombudsman was to be "a person of distinguished accomplishment in the field of law or public administration." His term was set at six years in order that it "not automatically begin and end

with the Office of the Mayor and the local governing
body." The Ombudsman was to investigate on complaint
or on his own initiative and would have the power of
subpoena. He would be allowed to publish his opinion
and recommendations and obliged to submit "a detailed
annual report of his activities" to the Governor, the
Department of Community Affairs, the Mayor, and the local governing body.

Schiff noted that it would be possible to establish
an Ombudsman in Newark simply by local ordinance but that
in the absence of enabling state legislation, the office
could not be given subpoena power. Stressing the need
to get the service to the people, Schiff suggested that
if an Ombudsman were created in Newark there should also
be at least three assistant Ombudsmen, each in charge of
a neighborhood storefront office.

Although the Addonizio-Schiff efforts to establish
an Ombudsman eventually came to nothing, there is no evidence that the two officials, both later indicted for
political corruption, were not seriously trying to create
a Newark office. Addonizio had come to Newark as a liberal reformer and an Ombudsman might have helped to pol-
ish up his rather tarnished liberal image; with OEO willing to foot the bill, the office would not cost the city
a penny, at least for a time. Besides these considerations, there was the need to mollify the Black leaders
calling for the implementation of the Hughes Report recommendation for a police review board without at the same
time offending the PBA. Finally, it is conceivable that
both men supported the Ombudsman in part because they
believed it would be a benefit to the citizens of Newark.

In any event, May 1968 found Norman Schiff in Tren-
ton supporting a proposal for a state Ombudsman but at
the same time urging the legislature first to pass enabling legislation to permit municipalities to appoint
Ombudsmen with subpoena power. On the basis of reports
in the Newark *Evening News* on May 9 and June 18 and 19,
it would appear that the failure to get the state legislature to pass such legislation--apparently needed to

4

secure OEO funding--killed the Addonizio Ombudsman plan. The last references in the press are accounts in June that the Mayor was directing his new Corporation Counsel Philip Gordon to draft a bill to give an urban Ombudsman subpoena powers. Until these powers were provided, Addonizio announced, no Newark Ombudsman would be appointed.


## Continued Discussion

After the collapse of the Addonizio proposal, the Ombudsman continued to be discussed in Newark. In October 1968, Emmett Godfrey of the Rutgers University Bureau of Community Affairs issued a 25 page report on the subject at the request of the city's Committee of Concern. The report, while cautioning against expecting too much from an Ombudsman, concluded that it "could and should be effective on small problems and minor issues." The experience of the OEO-financed Buffalo Ombudsman Project was described at some length as being especially relevant for Newark.

Late in the fall of 1969, a group of citizens formed an "*ad hoc* New Jersey Ombudsman Committee" and got 24 public and private organizations in the state to sponsor a New Jersey Ombudsman Conference in Newark on May 25, 1970. About 125 persons listened to the Swedish Ombudsman Alfred Bexelius, Walter Gellhorn, and others discuss the nature of the Ombudsman and the desirability of introducing the office into New Jersey. Small groups of participants continued the discussion of the latter question.[6] Clearly there was sufficient public discussion of the Ombudsman among Newark's attentive elites just prior to the Gibson administration to assure that at least some of its members were aware of the possible advisability of a Newark Ombudsman.

## A VARIETY OF COMPLAINT HANDLERS

When Kenneth Gibson took office as Mayor there were, of course, some complaint handlers already in existence in Newark:  the government agencies them- selves, the Mayor's office, municipal councilmen, the Human Rights Commission, and a recently established legal aid organization.  Complaints received by the Mayor's office were sent to the Business Administrator, who presumably made enquiries to the agencies involved.[7] Councilmen used their extensive connections in City Hall to assist constituents with problems there.

The Human Rights Commission was established by ordinance in 1952, and consists at present (1974) of 15 non-paid members appointed for 5 year terms by the Mayor; with a staff of 37 headed by an Executive Direc- tor.  Among its varied activities, the commission daily receives from Newark's citizens complaints of discrim- ination, especially regarding housing and employment.[8]

Newark's legal aid service was established with OEO funding to bring legal assistance to the poor. Al- though most of the assistance concerns non-governmental matters, its six neighborhood offices do receive each year a number of government related cases, welfare com- plaints being especially prominent.[9]

Mayor Gibson has added to these complaint channels an organization of community offices to assist citizens in their relations with the city government, a "Meet Your Mayor" night, and a free newspaper, which among other things publicizes complaint channels.

## Action Now:  Dispenser of Information

Action Now, a complaint referral organization founded with Model City funds on July 1, 1971, includes a central office in the basement of City Hall and a storefront office in each of the city's five wards. Citizens may call personally at these offices or use a 24 hour telephone service. When inaugurating the program, Gibson described the staff of the five centers as composed of "experts in administration and people knowledgeable about the needs of the community in which they will serve."[10] The knowledgeability seems based on staff being recruited for the centers from the neighborhoods they serve. The expression "experts in administration" was certainly an exaggeration, for whatever expertise the staff may have is acquired mainly on the job through information supplied by the central office and experience with handling clients.

Although bearing a superficial resemblance to an Ombudsman, Action Now in practice operates as a different type of organization. Its major activity is dispensing information. During its first year, it received 86,505 communications from the public; 93 percent were requests for information.[11] Even the 6,299 communications that might be characterized as complaints are usually not handled as an Ombudsman would handle them. Generally, complaints received by Action Now are referred to the public or private agency involved, with a later check to determine how the agency has responded. Sometimes Action Now staff go further and personally approach agencies to seek assistance for persons with problems. The office thus serves to put people in touch with government agencies or other organizations that can help them and to expedite the services. It does not appear to investigate complaints in the sense of trying to discover whether or not charges against abuses or defects in public agencies are correct.

Some Criticisms:  Action Now, and Human Rights Commission

It is impossible without further information to judge the success of Action Now. Certainly, the large input of requests for information and complaints suggests that it is helping to satisfy a social need hitherto neglected. Whatever its actual success, it has not been a success in the eyes of city councilmen, and some members of the Mayor's office also are not happy with its performance.

Criticism is aimed not so much at what it does as at what it does not do. The city's Business Administrator Cornelius Bodine, Jr., complained to the writer that Action Now did not use its experience to supply him with information about where major administrative weaknesses were to be found. According to Joseph Bradley, liaison officer for the Municipal Council in its relations with the Mayor, officials at City Hall objected to Action Now's frequently taking credit for settling complaints which in fact government agencies were already in the process of handling. He also related that councilmen were very dissatisfied with the operations of both Action Now and the Human Rights Commission. As evidence of the deficiencies of the former, he said that councilmen had told him that they were receiving more complaints now than before the new organization went into operation.[12]

Bradley's linking of Action Now with the Human Rights Commission in common failure was repeated independently by two councilmen interviewed by the writer. Michael P. Bottone and Sharpe James[13] also commented that Action Now sent complainants on to councilmen for help instead of settling their difficulties. Councilman James further accused both Action Now and the Human Rights Commission of being controlled by the Mayor,[14] and Councilman Bottone described the commission as having been turned by Gibson into a public relations organization. The latter remark possibly was provoked by the active part taken by the commission's Director Daniel W. Blue, Jr., in organizing Gibson's "Meet Your Mayor Night."

Significantly with respect to council attitudes towards an Ombudsman proposal, both councilmen held the position that Newark had no need for another complaint referral organization. The majority of Newark councilmen seemed to interpret the experience of Action Now and the Human Rights Commission as demonstrating

that the two institutions worked poorly and that there
was no need for a further similar institution which
would also be a failure.


## "Meet Your Mayor Night"

In February 1972, Mayor Gibson opened up still another channel through which Newark citizens might com-
plain of government action or inaction when he held his
first "Meet Your Mayor Night." The idea for such eve-
nings came from Blue, who continues to take an active
part in organizing them. As described in the newspaper
*Information* (August 21, 1972, p. 11),

> Almost every Tuesday night the mayor
> goes before a crowd gathered in a
> school, church, housing development,
> tavern, club, or recreation center.
> ...The mayor covers every ward in
> the city, since every meeting is
> held in a different section weekly.
> He is now well into his third swing
> around Newark.
>
> The sessions are usually arranged
> by civic, social and fraternal organ-
> izations. Their spokesmen question
> the mayor on problems and issues in-
> fluencing their everyday lives. Usu-
> ally there are high-ranking city offi-
> cials there who can answer any ques-
> tion that the mayor himself cannot
> answer....
>
> Complaints about specific situations
> are usually referred to department
> heads or to Rev. Ralph Grant, director
> of ACTION NOW, for follow-up after the
> meetings.

The Mayor is keen to have his senior officials attend
these meetings and shows his displeasure if they do not
appear.

On Tuesday, October 31, 1972, the writer observed
a well-attended Mayor's Night in the parish hall of a
Roman Catholic church in white middle-class Vailsburg.
Citizens raised several specific complaints, which the
Mayor referred to appropriate department heads while
promising quick consideration and action.[15]  Although
individual complaints were received, it was clear that
the meeting also functioned as a forum in which the
Mayor, in response to questions from the audience,
could defend his administration.

Thus, even more than Action Now, the "Meet Your
Mayor Night" can be perceived not only as a means for
exerting citizen influence on government but also as
a means by which the Mayor can build citizen support.
Interestingly, at the Vailsburg "Night" those conspic-
uously present included Michael Bottone, Councilman
for the area (West Ward) and Michael Bontempo, a Councilman-at-Large, who both appeared to use the meeting
for their own political purposes.  Bontempo took the
opportunity to deliver a rather lengthy speech from
the audience, while Bottone, who is shy of speaking
before audiences, was busy in private conversations.

## Information:  A Newspaper

The mixture of motives that seems to lie behind
the Mayor's Night is also evident with regard to the
newspaper *Information*.  It is published from time to
time by the Newark Office of Public Information, an
agency set up early in 1972 and financed by funds from
the federal Department of Housing and Urban Development
(HUD) and the New Jersey Department of Community Affairs.  Sixty thousand free copies of the first edi-
tion (August 1, 1972) were distributed throughout the
city with the assistance of the Community Development
Administration.  Issues describe various city programs,

provide names and addresses of city agencies, and include accounts of Action Now cases. Special columns in each issue are directed towards Blacks, Italians, and Puerto Ricans--the city's main ethnic groups. As would be expected, *Information* has been perceived by some city councilmen as still another electioneering device of the Mayor.

## IMPETUS FOR THE OMBUDSMAN

That the Ombudsman got as far as he did in Newark is the result of the combined efforts of the Mayor's Office and the Office of Economic Opportunity. About a year before Kenneth Gibson became Mayor, interest within OEO in funding experimental Ombudsmen quickened with the appointment of Donald Rumsfeld as director of the agency.

Rumsfeld, as a Republican congressman, had earlier sponsored Ombudsman legislation. He directed the OEO's Office of Program Development (OPD) to consider the possibility of testing several types of Ombudsmen to determine which would be of most use to the poor. The job of working up the programs was given to a program analyst in the Community Development Division of OPD, Gordon Wilcox, who energetically pushed them along.[16] He and others gave consideration to the classical Ombudsman, and were strongly influenced by the ideas of Walter Gellhorn, who was perceived as the leading American expert on the subject.[17]

## An Opportunity for Testing

In preparing for the fiscal year 1971 (beginning July 1, 1970), officials in the Community Development Division discussed the fact that Ombudsmen had not been tried in the most difficult settings--urban centers and heavily populated states--and agreed to look for an opportunity for such tests. Given this outlook, they were bound to look favorably upon any suggestion for

11

funding an Ombudsman in Newark. Indeed, it would have
been difficult to find a more arduous testing place.


## A Tepid Interest

The circumstances surrounding the sponsoring of
an Ombudsman by Gibson's administration cast some light
on the eventual failure of the project. According to
Kenneth Gibson, before the 1970 elections he and other
Black leaders had spoken of the possibility of an Ombudsman.[18]  Professor Stanley B. Winters, a friend and
supporter of the Mayor, wrote during the summer of 1971
that among Gibson's "tentative ideas" for Newark was
"a new department of investigation, independent of the
Mayor's office, to check on honesty in government."[19]

Immediately following his election, Gibson created
under Robert Curvin a transitional office to help his
new administration get under way. Among the tasks assigned to this office was that of drawing up a "shop-
ping list" which the Mayor would take with him on his
first trip to Washington in the spring of 1970 to seek
federal assistance for Newark. One of the items on the
list was a federally funded Ombudsman.[20]  Nothing, however, came of the Ombudsman proposal, primarily, it
would seem, because Wilbur Parker, who was given the
job of drafting a detailed plan, never carried out the
assignment. Parker has been described by an observer
of Newark politics as a procrastinator who also was
loath to offend politicians who would be able to prevent his appointment as Secretary to the Board of Education. By drafting an Ombudsman plan Parker was hardly likely to ingratiate himself with city councilmen,
some of whom, according to Winters, had told the Mayor
during this period that they would not approve such an
organization.[21]  Significantly, Gibson did nothing to
spur Parker to act or to put the planning for the Ombudsman into other hands. Such mayoral inaction appears to indicate that Gibson's commitment to the Ombudsman was not very high at this time.

## The OEO Initiative

Movement within the Gibson administration towards establishing an Ombudsman had ceased when early in February 1971, OEO took the initiative and sent Patricia Stolfa to meet with the Newark Community Development Administration (CDA) to propose an OEO-funded Ombudsman. When informed by his aides that the CDA showed little interest in the proposal, the Mayor decided that his office would cooperate with OEO in founding the institution. In light of Gibson's previous interest in the Ombudsman idea, his decision is understandable.

OEO had proposed funding a two-year demonstration project in Newark to round out its current experimentation with Ombudsmen. As one of the documents in the later grant application put it, "The wide scope, special nature and advanced state of Newark's urban crisis will provide the acid test of this concept. If an Ombudsman is effective in Newark, then it can be of value on the local level almost anywhere else." The motives of the Mayor's office in accepting the project appear to have been somewhat different from those of OEO. One of the Mayor's aides at that time relates,

> Because of the difficulty in controlling both the remnants of the Addonizio machine and the new breed of hustler, we thought an independent investigator would be extremely helpful. The complaint side of the Ombudsman did not excite us as much [as it did OEO]. We had just set up "Action Now" offices around the city which were to handle complaints and which were accountable to the Mayor's Office. As we envisioned him, the Ombudsman was to involve himself only in the most chronic citizen complaints, using the Action Now system to sift out less important complaints while the greater part of his effort would be devoted to uncovering corruption.[22]

In writing to accept OEO's offer, Gibson agreed
"to support the creation of an independent Office of
Municipal Ombudsman along OEO guidelines in so far as
the New Jersey State Law permits."[23] While OEO does
not appear to have established formal guidelines, its
officials were determined that the Newark experiment
follow very closely the Gellhorn model statute. Money
would be available only on the following condition:

> No funds will be released until the
> grantee has submitted to OEO/OPD
> written evidence that the Office of
> Municipal Ombudsman has been estab-
> lished either through passage of an
> Ordinance or the enactment of an
> Executive Order substantially re-
> flective of the model Ombudsman
> statute of Walter Gellhorn.

The insistence on the Gellhorn statute was later to
delay the drafting of the Newark ordinance, a delay
that may have contributed to the eventual failure of
the whole scheme.

## Budget and Salaries

The Mayor's office submitted its application to
OEO early in March 1971. $150,000 would be required
for the first year, the total cost for the two year
period being projected at $261,900. The form the
Ombudsman was to take resulted from collaboration between officials in the Mayor's office and OEO as well
as certain outside pressures. Besides the Ombudsman
himself, there were to be two assistants, an executive
secretary, two clerk typists, and a half-time investi-
gator.

The Ombudsman's salary, originally anticipated at
$25,000 a year, was set at $30,000, with each assistant to receive an annual salary of $17,000. In jus-
tifying the Ombudsman's salary, an OEO official ex-

plained to a superior, "The salary of an Ombudsman has been one of the means by which we seek to establish his stature and secure top quality candidates. In general, the salary is made equivalent to that of the highest judge within the jurisdiction."

Here again, OEO was following Gellhorn's advice, but, as the official noted, in Newark, the salary of the highest judge was not "an entirely adequate yardstick." The reason was that municipal judges in Newark received only $17,500 a year, half of what was earned by the Mayor and New Jersey state judges. To arrive at the $30,000 salary for the Ombudsman, the salary of the Mayor, municipal and state judges, as well as the $20,000 to $30,000 received by the city department heads and the $10,000 half-time salaries of city councilmen were all taken into account.

## Executive Order, City Ordinance or Council Resolution?

Interestingly, the question of just how the Ombudsman was to be established was not answered in the grant application. Documents prepared by OEO officials and the Mayor's office, however, suggest that the two organizations had different ideas about the matter. Thus an OEO "Highlight Memorandum" on the Newark project states,

> The Newark Municipal Ombudsman will be based on either an Executive Order or a city ordinance reflective of the model ombudsman statute in essential details. Although experience with executive ombudsmen has not been entirely happy, the former course of action may well be the stronger in this case, because the Mayor can delegate by Executive Order his right to information, while subpoena power cannot be transferred by ordinance.

Attached to this memorandum, however, was a statement prepared by the Mayor's office which declared, "The Municipal Council will advise and consent to the appointment of the Mayor to (sic) the Office of Municipal Ombudsman. The Ombudsman will submit his reports to this body as well as to the Mayor."

In July 1971, the question of the legality of not establishing the Ombudsman by ordinance was considered by Dennis Drasco of the Newark Corporation Counsel's office. He concluded in a memorandum dated July 29th,

> Adoption by the Council whether by Ordinance or Resolution is the only means available for the establishment of an Ombudsman. If the federal money does not pass through the city treasury a resolution would satisfy the statute. However, this avenue would prohibit inclusion of civil service status for the staff since this permanent status would extend beyond the federal grant.

Thus, Mayor Gibson was given no choice, since the advice of his legal office obliged him to seek council approval for his Ombudsman.

While he could have avoided proceeding by ordinance, the use of a council resolution would have raised additional problems and still not have allowed him to circumvent the council altogether. Councilmen could have used a resolution approving receipt of federal money as an opportunity to block the Ombudsman or to insist on various conditions. One cannot, however, rule out the possibility that such a resolution might have slipped through the council, which might have been less aware of its implications than those of a detailed ordinance.

Patricia Stolfa, the OEO official most directly involved in the Newark project, had fully expected the

Ombudsman to be established by executive order. When
she received word from Ira Jackson, her counterpart in
the Mayor's office, that an ordinance would be used,
she raised the ominous question, "Will its passage be
politically manageable?"[24] According to Philip Douglas,
the Mayor's office was fully aware of the hostility
councilmen were likely to feel towards the Ombudsman
proposal. "We, from the first, told OEO not to get
their hopes up too high on this project ultimately
getting through the Council."[25]

## The Ombudsman's Relationship to
## Action Now

The relationship the Ombudsman would have with
Action Now was critically important. As discussed in
several application documents at some length, Action
Now was depicted as complementing and assisting the
success of the Ombudsman. It would handle the large
number of routine complaints that deluge some urban
executive Ombudsmen and would refer to the Ombudsman
only those cases requiring careful impartial investigation. The Ombudsman, on the other hand, would refer
relatively trivial complaints to Action Now. According
to the "Highlight Memorandum" quoted above,

> A unique feature of this demonstra-
> tion, though not a part of the pro-
> ject itself, is the presence of the
> "Action Now" offices in the city.
> These offices, with five neighbor-
> hood locations, will also function
> as complaint handling mechanisms,
> but with an advocacy role and an
> outreach function whereby agency
> personnel can be present to hear
> the complaints of citizens. It is
> expected that "Action Now" offices
> will serve a referral function and
> also provide valuable data by which
> the Ombudsman can facilitate his
> reform role.

Another document lays special stress on the effect Action Now would have in freeing the Ombudsman from "the more routine duties of complaint-routing and providing information." It quotes with approval the following statement from the report to OEO on the Buffalo Ombudsman project: "Except for the purpose of gaining experience, an Ombudsman office should not function as an information or complaint-routing office. These functions can be more economically performed by a central office within the municipality."

Given the later misunderstanding in Newark in the Municipal Council and elsewhere concerning the relationship between the Ombudsman and Action Now, it needs to be stressed that those who hoped to introduce an Ombudsman into Newark did not intend the office to be a referral service or to take on an enormous load of trivial complaints. The Ombudsman was not expected to accept every complaint, but to spend his time on "the more general concerns of governmental administration." According to the job description, from which the phrase came,

> Normally, the Ombudsman will see to
> it that all complaints he receives
> have been channeled through the in-
> ternal mechanisms of the various city
> agencies. Normally, this would mean
> that many complaints will be referred
> to Action Now; however, at the Ombuds-
> man's discretion, any original griev-
> ance may be acted on without referral
> to the appropriate agency.

How this significant experiment in linking a classical Ombudsman with a referral agency would have worked in practice, we cannot know. Norman Abrams, a Gibson aide in charge of the Ombudsman project in its later phases, suggested to the writer that a representative of Action Now might have had an office adjacent to that of the Ombudsman, whose staff could rapidly and conveniently refer to Action Now people visiting the Ombudsman's office with small complaints or requests for information. Most complaints and enquiries probably would have come to the Ombudsman by phone, and those more appropriate for Action Now could easily have been switched to that office.

## Initial Opposition Easily Overcome

As part of the standard procedures for applying for an OEO grant, Mayor Gibson sent copies of the application for comment to Alvin Oliver, Executive Director of the United Community Corporation (the local Newark community action agency) and to James D. Coffee, Director of the New Jersey State Office of Economic Opportunity. Oliver did not respond to the communication, but on March 26th Coffee replied negatively. Although federal OEO officials had been actively involved in the preparation of the Newark Ombudsman project, Coffee, who was also Assistant Commissioner for the New Jersey Department of Community Affairs, appears not to have been even consulted until this time. In his letter to the Washington OEO office, he recognized that Newark required all the help it could get but did not believe that the city or its citizens would be assisted by an Ombudsman. As far as he could see, the proposed Ombudsman would simply duplicate the work of Action Now and was a superficial, inadequate attempt to deal with the city's problems.

Coffee's opposition, the first to be encountered by the Ombudsman, was easily swept aside. In replying to Coffee's letter, Joe P. Maldonado, Assistant Director of the OEO Office of Program Development, observed that Coffee had failed to understand the difference between a classical Ombudsman and an organization such as Action Now. Answering the charge that an Ombudsman would not help the inhabitants of Newark, Maldonado remarked, "As for the benefit to the citizens of Newark, I believe we must rely on the opinion of their major elected official, Mayor Gibson, who has sought and endorsed the Ombudsman project."

## Search for a Candidate

During the summer of 1971, work began in Newark both on drafting an Ombudsman ordinance and on preparing for the selection of a well qualified person to fill the office. At this stage, the Ombudsman Activities Project (OAP) and in particular Professor Stanley V. Anderson, its director and a leading academic authority on Ombudsmen, became involved. The OAP had been funded by OEO to monitor, evaluate, and lend advisory assistance to its Ombudsman projects. On July 13th, Anderson and Patricia Stolfa of OEO met in Newark with officials from the Mayor's office. At this time the Mayor's aide in charge of developing an Ombudsman plan was Ira A. Jackson, a white Harvard graduate, originally from Massachusetts. During his visit with Jackson, Anderson offered to pay (from OAP's grant from OEO), $1500 to finance an expert committee picked from the New York metropolitan area to nominate a suitable candidate for Ombudsman. The offer was accepted.

Mayor Gibson appointed to the search committee James Paul, Dean of the Rutgers Law School; Raymond A. Brown, a Black Jersey City attorney prominent in New Jersey civil rights and criminal cases; and Ronald Haughton, Director of the Board of Mediation and Community Disputes of New York City. The committee, which first met on July 29th, did not produce a candidate until late in the fall, after considering 50 possibilities and interviewing ten persons.

The committee's choice finally fell upon Earl Phillips, the 38-year-old Black President of the Essex County Urban League. A graduate of Newark's South Side High School, Phillips had gone on to receive a B.A. in Psychology and History from Howard University in 1961 and an M.A. in Community Relations, Counseling, and Guidance from Columbia University in 1962. During much of the decade prior to his nomination, he had been active in community relations work--especially community-police relations--in New Jersey. Ira Jackson reported to Stolfa and Anderson that the Search Committee and the Mayor's office were very enthusiastic about Phillips. For their part, Stolfa and Anderson had some misgivings. The former was worried whether Phillips, who had no experience in either law or government, was properly qualified to be an Ombudsman. She noted that all American Ombudsmen had one or the other qualification, which she believed to be important. In Anderson's view, the absence of education or experience in law or government was a shortcoming but not a disqualification. However, while noting that on paper Phillips's qualifications were impressive, Anderson was concerned that the Search Committee and the Mayor's office were thinking in terms of a mediator or troubleshooter rather than a classical Ombudsman. While they had such reservations, Stolfa and Anderson did not think it appropriate to voice them in Newark.

## The Ombudsman Ordinance

After the determination in July by the Corporation Counsel's Office that the Ombudsman proposal could not avoid action by the Municipal Council, work was begun on an ordinance by aides in the Mayor's office and Corporation Counsel lawyers. This group was faced with combining the principles of the Gellhorn Model Statute with the limitations New Jersey law places on authority exercized by municipalities. On December 1, 1971, Ira Jackson sent a draft of the Ombudsman ordinance to Stolfa and Anderson along with an announcement of Earl Phillips's nomination. His letter to Stolfa indicates that the Mayor's office hoped to have the Ombudsman in operation by the end of January. If the final form of the ordinance could be agreed upon by December 15th, it might be put before the Municipal Council on December 30th along with the Phillips nomination. "If all goes well," Jackson remarked, "the second reading will occur at the council's January 19th meeting, and our Ombudsman will be able to start setting up shop immediately afterwards."

Timing can be crucially important in determining the success or failure of a policy proposal. Had the Jackson time-table been adhered to, it is possible that the Newark Ombudsman would have succeeded. If, however, success had been possible, it would have been highly unlikely, because a major fight between the Mayor and the council blew up on January 5th before the second reading could take place.

As it was, the time-table had to be abandoned because OEO registered strong objections to the draft ordinance for not adhering closely enough to the Gellhorn model. When submitting the draft to Patricia Stolfa, Jackson had tried to anticipate such criticism by observing that "the ordinance as it reads at this time is the best version of the...[Gellhorn] statute we could hope to obtain in accordance with New Jersey law." Stolfa and her colleagues, however, decided that the statute would not do and immediately returned it to the Mayor's office along with a copy of the Gellhorn statute in which every passage missing in the Newark draft ordinance was underlined.

## Defects:   The OEO View

Stolfa found a number of defects in the draft. *First*, Section 1, "Definitions," did not expressly exempt courts from the Ombudsman's jurisdiction. *Second*, there was no section on the qualifications of the Ombudsman. *Third*, Section 3 of the draft provided that the Ombudsman, appointed by the Mayor with the advice and consent of the Municipal Council, was to have a four year term concurrent with that of the Mayor. In Stolfa's opinion, the minimally acceptable term was five years and the type of majority required for council approval should have been specified.

*Fourth*, Section 4 allowed the Mayor at his discretion to remove the Ombudsman from office; the council had power to prevent such a removal only by a 2/3 vote of its entire membership. Stolfa believed that an

Ombudsman should be removed only for disability or malfeasance and that the method of removal should be mod-
ified. *Fifth*, she felt that there was no need to re-
tain Section 9(e), which appeared to direct the Ombudsman to refer all complaints he did not investigate to
"an appropriate public or private agency."[26] *Sixth*,
Stolfa was concerned that Section 9, which dealt with
the powers of the Ombudsman, omitted the subpoena power. *Seventh*, also disquieting was the absence of any
legal immunity for the Ombudsman, which she believed
would be especially important in Newark. *Finally*, she
desired to have added to Section 6 dealing with the
Ombudsman's salary a "conflict of interest statement"
forbidding him to hold or be a candidate for any other
public office or to engage in any other occupation.[27]

On December 9th, Patricia Stolfa and Leonard
Slaughter met with Mayor Gibson in Newark to try to
arrive at agreement on an ordinance acceptable to OEO.
They still hoped to reach agreement in time to have
the ordinance submitted to the Municipal Council by
the December 15th date (earlier mentioned by Ira Jackson). At the meeting, Gibson did accept several
changes but explained that as much as he agreed with
OEO's desire to give the Newark Ombudsman subpoena
power, immunity from prosecution, and the power to
punish persons refusing to answer questions, New Jersey law simply did not allow municipalities to grant
such authority. The Mayor argued that the Ombudsman
would still be valuable to Newark without such powers
and that it was now up to OEO to decide whether or not
to accept the unavoidable limitations. Slaughter and
Stolfa replied that they very much wanted to establish
an Ombudsman in Newark but that they wanted the Mayor's
office to make further efforts to give the new office
at least subpoena power. The meeting ended with a determination to go forward but with postponement of a-
greement on the final form of the ordinance. The latter decision meant that the original time-table for
submitting the ordinance to the council had to be
scrapped.

The Mayor's office proceeded to consult further with Corporation Counsel and to correspond with operating American Ombudsmen to determine whether the latter had subpoena power and, if so, how they had managed to get it. The Mayor's aides concluded from their enquiries that the existing Ombudsmen had only in the rarest instances resorted to the use of their subpoena power but relied instead on their prestige, impartiality, and investigative skills to secure the information they required.[28] By January 13th, a somewhat revised ordinance, still omitting the subpoena power had been prepared. When asked his opinion of it, Stanley Anderson replied that it was "a first-rate statute,"[29] and the officials at OEO were prepared to accept that the ordinance was as close as Newark could get to the Gellhorn model. Thus, by the end of January 1972, there were no further differences between the Mayor's office and OEO to prevent the establishment of the Newark Ombudsman. Unfortunately, a far more formidable obstacle remained in the path of the Ombudsman: the bitter conflict between the Mayor and a large majority of the Municipal Council.

# II

## The Ombudsman and the
## Newark Municipal Council

### SOME COUNCIL ATTITUDES
### BLURRING RACIAL CLEAVAGES

Although journalists and scholars frequently stress
the prevalence and importance of racial conflict in Newark politics, race was not an important factor in the
defeat of the Ombudsman. The Municipal Council divides
less frequently along racial lines than the well publicized occasions of racial divisions would suggest. Since
ethnic considerations are important in determining votes
in Newark's non-partisan elections, it is not surprising
that the white and Black councilmen should be alert to
issues that might stir their respective supporters along
ethnic divisions. On the other hand, several factors work
against ethnic voting on the council. The three white
Councilmen-at-Large--Bontempo, Giuliano, and Villani--
and Earl Harris, the single Black Councilman-at-Large,
have to contend with an electorate rather evenly divided
between Black and white voters.[1] The same is true of
Councilman Michael P. Bottone of the racially balanced
West Ward, who maintains that in the 1970 elections he
did better in his Black than his white districts. Also
significant in blurring racial cleavages on the council
is the fact that Black and white councilmen, while divided to some degree by the ethnic differences, find
common interests by being members of the same organization. When a matter before the council is perceived as
adversely affecting their collective power or their
electoral strength, there is a tendency for Black and
white councilmen to close ranks against a mutual antag-

24

onist. Almost all of the councilmen have been raised
in Newark and in making their way in local politics
have come to accept the values and attitudes common to
Newark politicians. These shared values and attitudes
also would seem to contribute to moderating racial divisions.

Finally, with respect to Mayor-council relations,
the claims of racial brotherhood appear far weaker than
those of political ambition. Being a Black councilman
does not prevent a man who aspires to the mayoral office from frequently attacking the actions of an incum-
bent Black Mayor.


COUNCIL V. MAYOR

From the beginning of his administration, Mayor
Gibson has encountered difficulties in getting both
Black and white councilmen to support some of his most
important proposals. This inability of Mayor Gibson
and the Municipal Council to get on together was soon
well publicized in the press, and on November 9, 1971,
a New Jersey legislative task force on Newark's expenditure of state funds issued an interim report, which
among other things criticized the deleterious effects
of Mayor-council conflict on the government of the
city.[2]  In January 1972, Mayor-council relations de-
teriorated even further during a bitter dispute over
use of the first $1.2 million of a $7 million Model
Cities Planned Variations grant.

The attack on the Mayor's request for council acceptance of the funds was led by Sharpe James and Louis
Turco, both of whom were thought to be considering running for Mayor at the next elections. James, a Black
councilman, complained that the Mayor would have sole
authority in spending the money with the council being
given no role at all. He also strongly objected to
the rumored choice to head the agency which was to car-
ry out the city-wide Planned Variations programs. That
choice he believed to be Ira Jackson, an aide to the

Mayor who had come to Newark from Massachusetts and was characterized by James as "a poverty pimp--someone who jumps from one poverty program to another trying to take care of himself."[3]  This hostility towards outsiders who would take jobs away from Newark residents was shared by another Black councilman, Earl Harris, who referred to them as "glorified carpetbaggers."

Council President Louis M. Turco noted that $100,000 of the initial grant of federal money was to go for public relations, and commented, "This would give the Mayor, in this program alone, a bigger press office than the Governor of the State of New Jersey." Turco also complained about the expenditure of $250,000 for salaries of new officials to oversee the programs at a time when existing city services for the public were inadequate.  Mayor Gibson responded to this defeat by holding a news conference in which he branded councilmen with the charges of "demagoguery" and of attempting to usurp his appointing power.  It was not until February 15th that a compromise on Planned Variations was worked out between the Mayor and the council.

To understand why Mayor Gibson and the Municipal Council were unable to work smoothly together and, more particularly, why the council opposed the Ombudsman, some knowledge of Newark politics and Gibson's character and style is necessary.[4]

## THE NEWARK POLITICAL STYLE

Since the late 1920's when the businessmen who had hitherto been dominant in Newark politics began to move to the suburbs, City Hall has been dominated by a type of politician frequently found in older American cities.  Stanley Winters has described the typical city commissioner of the 1930's and 40's as

> a self-made man, usually from the
> lower middle class, closely identified

> with a specific ethnic, religious,
> or political group, and tending to
> speak for special interest rather
> than general welfare. These commis-
> sioners included dedicated men, but
> some maintained dubious links with
> racketeers; others engaged in finan-
> cial and real estate deals that
> raised suspicions of misuse of pub-
> lic office, if the many indictments
> and occasional convictions of Newark
> officials are reliable clues.[5]

This characterization of the later commission period of
Newark government applies equally well to the strong
Mayor-council government introduced in 1954. The record of corruption and concomitant administrative inefficiency of the Addonizio administration of 1962-70
is a clear indication that the style of Newark politics
had not changed. On the other hand, Mayor-council government did provide the occasion for frequent struggles
between the Mayor and the council over patronage and
the role each should play in policy-making and administration.

## The Struggle for Governmental Power

When Kenneth Gibson came to office in July 1970,
after campaigning to improve municipal services and to
eliminate corruption, he faced a council that saw him
as a competitor for governmental power and did not look
kindly on a proposal for an independent complaint hand-
ler. Whatever its legal role, the council was accustomed to influencing administrative decisions, including the allocation of jobs. In this respect, at least
two of the three new Black councilmen seem to side with
their white counterparts.[6]

By being able to influence the allocation of public jobs and the relations of city agencies with the
public, councilmen are able to strengthen their personal

electoral organizations and to please their constituents. Since Newark elections are non-partisan, party affiliations and appeals on public issues have little significance. It is to be expected, therefore, that councilmen intent on reelection should strive to build up voter support through available means, which include ethnic appeals and provision of services for supporters. Service to constituents is perceived by councilmen as a vital element in building voter support, and they are unlikely to be enthusiastic about proposals for new organizations that might offer competition. Also, accustomed to seeing various public offices used to increase electoral support and viewing the Mayor with considerable suspicion, councilmen find it difficult to accept the notion of a new public office being independent of both the Mayor and themselves. Rather they are inclined to view an official proposed and appointed by the Mayor as another cog in the Mayor's machine. Finally, any persons still on the council interested in increasing their incomes through political corruption might be concerned about a proposed organization whose investigations might lead back to them, even if legally they are excluded from its jurisdiction.

## The Mayor as "Technocratic Moralist"

It would be incorrect, however, to suggest that the failure since 1970 of the Municipal Council to cooperate with the Mayor can be explained solely in terms of the council, for Mayor Gibson's own personality and political style also have been influential.[7] Unlike his predecessors and most of the current members of the council, Kenneth Gibson is not a typical Eastern urban machine politician. Indeed, he has emphasized that he is no "politician" at all and appears to find it difficult to disguise his contempt for most of the councilmen whom he has publicly referred to as "demagogues" and "machine politicians" and who symbolize for him the corrupt and self-seeking traditional style of Newark politics he is striving to overcome.

While Gibson has been obliged to grant councilmen patronage with regard to some minor jobs, councilmanic attempts to influence major public appointments have been firmly and publicly rejected as improper efforts to usurp his power of appointment. He has no intention of sharing it with the council. From all accounts Mayor Gibson is a rather withdrawn man--a "loner"--at ease only with friends and neither very successful in nor much concerned about interpersonal relations. Negotiation, bargaining and compromise, which have played a large part in traditional urban politics in the United States, appear to be distasteful to him. In the opinion of Gustav Heningburg, the coordinator of Gibson's 1970 election campaign, "By temperament and by training he's an engineer accustomed to careful analysis....He's his own adviser. He listens and he absorbs and then he goes off somewhere to make decisions."[8] According to North Ward Councilman Frank Megaro, "There is no compromise with the Mayor. It's either yes or no for him, that's the way he sees it."

Gibson prefers to deal with councilmen at a distance, meeting with them only rarely when obliged by circumstances to seek their agreement. The private bi-monthly meetings between Mayor and council of the Addonizio administration have been discontinued. The staff Gibson has selected to assist him in policymaking have been chosen primarily for their intelligence and ability rather than as builders of political support. Policies that require council approval are believed by the Mayor to be beyond much compromise.* Should the

---

* Gibson's performance as Mayor of Newark is understandable in terms of a type of urban reformer who might be called the "technocratic moralist," a man who enters politics because of deep concern over what he perceives as the inefficiency, self-seeking, and corruption of the politicians in power. Such a man comes to office rather reluctantly because of a moral obligation to eliminate these shortcomings. He has a strong

council turn down his proposal, he is likely to conclude that his opponents must be acting from improper motives and consequently to hold them up to public scorn.

———————

sense of his own righteousness and little tolerance for the moral failings of others, including the established "politicians" whom he identifies (always with some reason) with the defects in his city's government.

The technocratic moralist generally arrives in public office after achieving a certain degree of business or professional success. This earlier experience-- as well as, possibly, other causes--inclines him towards the belief that there are rational solutions to various social and governmental problems discoverable through the careful application of intelligence and expertise.

In this respect, the technocratic moralist should be distinguished from other types of political reformers such as the "romantic dreamer" or the "inexperienced theoretician." The technocratic moralist is a practical man used to solving concrete problems of a technical sort not requiring negotiation. Believing greatly in the correctness of his solutions to problems, he tends to view persistent opposition to them as a sign of stupidity or immorality. Consequently he reacts to opposition with impatience, indignation and a disinclination to compromise differences. This aversion to compromise is heightened if opposition comes from the despised "politicians." Such a man, because of his intolerance of moral imperfection and an inability to "suffer fools gladly" and also, perhaps, because of having an introverted personality, is not at ease in his relations with any but his close friends and therefore lacks the surface warmth and geniality that other political leaders often use to win support. In addition, because of the high value he places on his own integrity and the importance of honest government, the technocratic moralist finds it distasteful to distribute material rewards from government sources in order to secure support for his election or policies. To win

## MOVES TOWARD ESTABLISHING
## AN OMBUDSMAN

In January 1972, the already poor relations between Mayor Kenneth Gibson and the Newark Municipal
Council worsened because of the quarrel over the
Planned Variations Program. Believing the intense
hostility of the council towards his administration
would prevent the passage of the Ombudsman ordinance
at this time, Gibson decided to postpone it.

A further difficulty arose in March when the
Mayor, uncertain that he would ever have an Ombudsman
office to which to appoint Earl Phillips and anxious
to bring him into his administration, appointed Phillips the director of the new High Impact Anti-Crime
Program, which was to receive $20 million in federal

---

such support, he is obliged to depend on gratitude for
the impersonal achievements of his administration, expectations of more of the same, and respect for his
and his administration's honesty and efficiency. Usually in the case of traditional American urban politicians, such respect, expectations or gratitude are not
sufficiently strong to guarantee their support. Although he enters office with a determination to set
public matters right, he often has only a short tenure
and leaves unfulfilled most of the goals that require
the cooperation of other public office holders. The
technocratic moralist can be expected to promote "good
government" reforms such as an Ombudsman; unfortunately,
in the traditional American urban setting he is not
well suited for achieving his objectives.[9]

Finally, the technocratic moralist might be expected to be the product of a middle or upper-middle
class home. He is, however, not unknown among self-
made men who have risen to middle class status from
working or lower-middle class backgrounds. Leo P.
Carlin, the last reforming Mayor of Newark before Gibson, is an excellent example. See Douglas, "Reform
in Newark," pp. 65-70.

funds. Thus, there arose the need to find a new candidate for Ombudsman, a problem which the Mayor decided not to handle until after the ordinance had been
passed.

## The City Clerk's View

In March, the Mayor decided to try his luck with
the council. To accompany the ordinance, Cornelius
Bodine, his Business Administrator, prepared a short
memorandum describing and praising the Ombudsman proposal and distinguishing its objectives from those of
Action Now. Bodine's, however, was not the only advice the council received about the Ombudsman. In Newark, the City Clerk, who serves as the council's clerk
and advises the council on the exercise of its legislative function, has for years been influential in city
government. The office of City Clerk, held by Harry
Reichenstein from 1933 to 1972, became the highest
paid position in city government; further, the clerk's
administrative assistants are paid far more than those
of the Mayor. Since the basis for Reichenstein's power
was the influence he exercised over the council, he
generally promoted the council's power rather than that
of the Mayor.[10] The clerk's office employs four analysts
to assist the council; the Chief Analyst, Irving Polster,
was known not to favor the idea of a Newark Ombudsman.

## First Reading of the Ordinance

As is so often the case with legislative time-
tables, the Ombudsman's dates slipped for one reason
or another: presentation of the ordinance to the
council was set for March 29th, postponed to April 5th
and then to May 3rd when the first reading finally occurred. Before the May reading, however, the council
at its April 19th meeting had agreed to accept the OEO
grant. As a condition for acceptance, it insisted on
the City Clerk's office being exempted from the Ombudsman's jurisdiction.[11] Because the clerk's office

functioned partly as an agent of the council, a case could be made for exemption; however, the office also carried on a number of purely administrative tasks, such as issuing marriage licenses, which an Ombudsman would be expected to have within his jurisdiction. Although not happy with the change, the Mayor's office and OEO agreed to accept the exemption in order to ease the passage of the ordinance.

From the standpoint of the measure's success, Dennis Westbrooks was the worst choice for a councilman to pilot the Ombudsman ordinance through the Municipal Council. This was not because he was insufficiently prepared, for he had taken time to read up on the subject and, as a result, had considerably better understanding of the nature of Ombudsmen than other councilmen. Nor can Westbrooks be faulted for not vigorously supporting the ordinance. Rather, his defect as the council's main Ombudsman advocate lay in the fact that he did not have strong ties with other councilmen, and at least some of the white councilmen perceived him as a dangerous Black militant. However, the Ombudsman had so little support on the council that it is doubtful whether any other councilman would have been prepared to sponsor the proposal. Councilman Harris, who seconded the motion during the first and second readings, was at best lukewarm in his support.[12]

The motion to adopt the Ombudsman ordinance passed its first reading on May 3rd by a comfortable majority of 6 to 2 with one abstention.[13] On this occasion, only Councilman Anthony J. Giuliano is recorded in the minutes as having spoken unequivocally against the Ombudsman, a position from which he never wavered during council consideration of the proposal. According to the former president of the PBA, the Ombudsman was an unnecessary duplication of work that should be done by the Mayor, the Business Administrator, the Human Rights Commission, and other existing local government agencies. Giuliano is not recorded as making any connection between the Ombudsman and a civilian police review

board during this or any other council meeting, although he may have had such a connection in mind when
he referred to "his experience with men of this sort
who come in and add confusion, harass employees and
decent citizens..."[14]

While Giuliano was the only councilman to speak
out squarely against the Ombudsman, Dennis Westbrooks
was the only one to speak up clearly in his favor.
Much of the discussion turned on the narrower issue
of the Ombudsman's term, with Councilmen Turco and
Megaro arguing that it was too long. Turco maintained
that the term should end in 1974 when elections might
produce a new Mayor or new councilmen who would prefer
another person to occupy the office. If the ordinance
were amended to reduce the term to two years, he pro-
mised to support it. Frank G. Megaro, who was to vote
against the Ombudsman on all possible occasions, spoke
in support of a one-year term, arguing that it was a
new office, which, if successful, could be continued
for a second year.[15] In answer to these proposals to
shorten the Ombudsman's term, Westbrooks contended that
the office was not a political position and should not
be treated as such, an argument in which Councilman
Bontempo concurred.

The discussion ended in a manner which, from hind-
sight, seems ominous. Giuliano spoke a second time,
among other things objecting to "creating another mon-
strosity in City Hall," which probably was an allusion
to Action Now. He was followed by Earl Harris, who,
according to the minutes, said, "The City Clerk mentioned the fact that we have the right to approve this
appointee and by exercising wisdom we can make a determination whether the individual nominee measures up to
our standards, and having that sort of power we should
move expeditiously on the vote."

Were these remarks a message to councilmen that
they could avoid responsibility for voting against the
ordinance yet reserve the opportunity to destroy the
Ombudsman at the nomination stage? Such an interpre-

tation receives some support from a remark made by
Joseph Bradley, the council's liaison with the Mayor's
office. Bradley, who had been told by Louis Turco to
talk with the writer during his visit to Newark in November 1972, related that when the ordinance had been put
before the council in May, councilmen were told that
passage did not preclude their changing their minds
about having an Ombudsman when the office came to be
filled.[16]

## Second Reading and Vote to Pass

When the second reading and vote on the final
passage of the ordinance took place on May 17th, again
only Councilman Giuliano spoke in opposition. The Ombudsman was an unnecessary duplication of work already
being done by others, and the money could be better
spent "to keep career employees on the job." At the
end of the second reading, the council's vote went as
at the end of the first, except that Council President
Turco slid off the fence and voted against the ordinance.

## A List of Candidates

The ordinance having been accepted by the council,
Marvin McGraw, a Mayor's aide, began to compile a new
list of possible candidates for Ombudsman by asking
for suggestions from members of the former search committee, Earl Phillips, and others. In July, a committee composed of Norman Abrams, McGraw, and the Corporation Counsel William Walls met and chose from a list
of twelve names four persons to be interviewed. A little later, two other possibilities were proposed and
they were interviewed as well.

Among the six interviewees were two local men who
had some support among some of the white councilmen.
Joseph A. Frisina had been appointed Deputy Mayor by
Gibson in return for the backing he had received during

the 1970 election. There was nothing in his professional background to qualify him as an Ombudsman and
his lack of activity as Deputy Mayor suggests that he
also would not have been an energetic Ombudsman. Roger
A. Lowenstein, Assistant Corporation Counsel since
1970 and a young man anxious to become the Newark Ombudsman, had much in his background to recommend him
for the job. The son of Alan V. Lowenstein, a prominent Newark civic reformer of the 1950's, Roger Lowenstein graduated from Harvard Law School *cum laude* in
1968. His active role in the civil rights movement
during the 1960's should have made him more acceptable
to the Black councilmen than many other white candidates. To the extent that racial considerations might
be involved, his being neither Black nor of Italian
origin was a disadvantage that could have become an
advantage had the two major ethnic groups been unable
to agree on a candidate. In office he would have appeared more impartial than a person with ethnic links
to either the Black or Italian communities. During
the writer's interview with him, Councilman Bottone
without prompting expressed the belief that Lowenstein
would have made an excellent Ombudsman. He may have
been less popular with councilmen carried over from
the Addonizio era, because as Assistant Corporation
Counsel he had been involved in getting a $40,000 re-
fund for the city. The sum had been paid to the Hu-
mane Society as the result of what Lowenstein considered to be the fraudulent conflict of interest of two
councilmen.

## Ranking the Candidates

Why was the apparently well-qualified Lowenstein
not nominated to be Ombudsman? Several factors appear
to have influenced the Mayor not to nominate him. First,
the nominating committee ranked Robert Washington above
Lowenstein as the best candidate for Ombudsman. Because
Gibson highly respected William Walls's opinion, he was
not likely to pass over Washington, especially with
Lowenstein coming from the Corporation Counsel's Office.
Once the Mayor perceived Washington as the most qualified

candidate, he refused to compromise on anyone else for fear that this would open the door to council control over his power of appointment.

Second, although Gibson had instructed the nominating committee to find the best man and had not mentioned color, the committee itself was unanimously agreed that the Ombudsman should be Black. This appears to have been the only occasion when racial considerations affected the outcome of the efforts to establish a Newark Ombudsman, and it is quite possible that the committee would have recommended Washington even if race had not been involved. Third, and especially important after the council refused to accept Washington, was Gibson's belief that Lowenstein had acted improperly in trying to secure the office for himself. Not satisfied with asking the Mayor to appoint him, the ambitious young man approached several councilmen to seek support. In doing the latter, he overplayed his hand, for news of his private meetings with councilmen to obtain their backing was not likely to endear him to Mayor Gibson. The Mayor was inclined to suspect the worst of such ambitious office seeking and of anything involving the council. He may also have concluded that Lowenstein was secretly trying to get the council to reject Washington in order to clear the way for himself.

## Gibson's Choice: Washington

Robert B. Washington's credentials were certainly impressive. A lawyer, Black and 30 years old, residing in Chevy Chase, Maryland, he was legal counsel to the U.S. Senate Committee on the District of Columbia, a lecturer on legal process and administrative law at Catholic University, and recently had been a teaching fellow at Harvard Law School.[17] In just about every way Washington, who had been recommended to the second search committee by Dean James Paul of the Rutgers Law School, was an excellent choice to be the first Newark Ombudsman. He was, however, to have one grave defect in the eyes of some councilmen. Although a native of

Newark, Washington had not resided in New Jersey since
the summer of 1968, and this five years' absence led to
his being perceived by two of the Black councilmen as
an outsider who was using the Ombudsman's office as a
stepping stone in his professional career and taking
the job away from a Newark resident.

Having picked his Ombudsman, Gibson planned to put
Washington's name before the Municipal Council on September 6th. At this time, Norman Abrams was optimistic
about the chances of the nomination being accepted by
the council, which seemed to him to be less hostile to
the Ombudsman than it had been in the past. With Business Administrator Bodine's assistance, Abrams was look-
ing about for suitable office space outside of City Hall
to house the Ombudsman and his staff. Gibson postponed
the September 6th date for putting Washington's name
before the council when he discovered that some of the
councilmen he was most depending on would be absent.
When the nomination was presented on September 20th,
councilmen voted to defer action until they had had an
opportunity to interview the candidate.

By this time, Abrams's optimism of the first of
the month had faded, and he described Mayor-council relations to the writer by phone on the 21st as very de-
pressing. Rumors in City Hall at this time were that
the council was opposed to Washington because he was an
outsider and some councilmen talked of wanting Deputy
Mayor Frisina. According to one story, an unofficial
vote during a private session of the council had gone
8 to 1 against Washington. With such a bleak prospect
for Washington, Mayor Gibson took a decision that must
have been unpleasant for him. He would go before the
Tuesday private session of the council to defend his
candidate.

Mayor and Council Face to Face

The Mayor's meeting with the Municipal Council on
October 3rd convinced him that the Washington nomination

had little chance of success.[18]  Councilman Giuliano
opened the discussion by asking whether Joseph Frisina,
who he said had a good record, had been considered. The
Mayor replied that Frisina had been considered by the
search committee along with 15 other candidates but
that Washington was the best qualified of all.  To rebut the criticism that his candidate was an outsider,
he stressed that Washington had been born and raised
in Newark and, indeed, had gone to the same high school
as some of the councilmen.  When asked whether Washington had been admitted to the New Jersey Bar, he replied
affirmatively.  President Turco countered by observing
that Washington had not worked in Newark for eight
years, but it was pointed out to him that Washington
had served in the Newark Legal Services Project in the
summer of 1968.  At this point the Mayor declared it
was his view and that of OEO that the Ombudsman should
not be identified with local politics or the current
administration.  Washington was as close as one could
go in selecting a local candidate without jeopardizing
the success of the office.  Giuliano asked whether this
was why Frisina had not been nominated and was told that
it was one of the reasons.

President Turco changed the direction of the council's attack by again raising the issue of the Ombudsman's five year term.  When he argued that a new administration and council should be allowed to appoint a
new Ombudsman, the discussion took an ominous turn, for
Turco was now questioning not the qualifications of the
candidate but a part of the ordinance the council had
accepted four and a half months before.  Gibson responded by again insisting that the Ombudsman should be
above politics and reminded the council that OEO had
insisted on a five year term as part of the funding a-
greement.  Although the new City Clerk Frank D'Ascensio
explained that the wording of the ordinance did not com-
mit the city to paying for the Ombudsman after the two
year OEO grant ran out, Turco continued to insist on
the term's ending in 1974.  He had, he said, voted
against the ordinance because of the five year term and
he would vote against any candidate who would serve for

that period. Councilman Bontempo suggested that the
Mayor appoint Washington for only two years, to which
Gibson replied that he had no intention of following
anything but the law which required five years.

Mayor Gibson's reaction to the position the council appeared to be developing was revealed in his response to Turco's remark that the council was keeping
the Ombudsman issue quiet in order to avoid embarrassing Gibson and Washington. According to Abrams's account,

> The Mayor retorted by insisting that
> there was no embarrassment for him or
> Washington. He wanted the thing in
> the open and he wanted the Council to
> say yes or no. He insisted that, as
> city ordinance directs, they had to
> act publicly on his nominee and he
> wanted them to do that. "If you don't
> want an Ombudsman," he said, "we'll
> let OEO take the money to another
> city."

The meeting ended with some councilmen suggesting that
before a decision was made they wanted to interview
Washington. The proposal was accepted by the council.
Mayor Gibson left the private meeting extremely pessimistic about the chances of Washington's acceptance by
the council.

Although positive action by the council seemed unlikely, efforts continued within the Mayor's office to
save the Ombudsman. Newspapers were approached for
backing, and on October 17th the *Star-Ledger* carried
an editorial supporting the "needed watchdog" and de-
fending it against the opposition of the two policemen's organizations which, as the newspaper said, had
"suddenly surfaced." Because councilmen wanted proof
that OEO was insisting on a five year term for the Ombudsman, Norman Abrams phoned Ira Kaye in Washington

for such evidence.[19] At this stage, however, these
efforts were too little and too late, and events continued to develop after October 3rd to make the defeat
of the Ombudsman even more likely.


## Attitude Toward Outsiders

It has been shown that some councilmen were strongly adverse to hiring outsiders for public positions in
Newark, and that questions had been raised about Washington. Shortly after the October 3rd meeting, Bailus
Walker, Jr., Director of the Newark Department of
Health and Welfare, announced unexpectedly that he was
resigning in November to accept a senior position in
the federal Department of Health, Education and Welfare
(HEW). Walker had come to Newark from Cleveland less
than nine months before and this fact further inflamed
feeling within the Municipal Council against outsiders.
When Walker's nomination had come before the council
in January, Councilman Earl Harris voted against it.
He explained his vote by saying that while he did not
question Walker's qualifications or the Mayor's right
to nominate the directors of his government departments,
he could not support the nomination because he strongly
opposed appointments of non-residents and believed that
a qualified director could have been found among Newark
residents. Councilman James also had disagreed with
the Mayor's choosing a director from Cleveland but felt
compelled to accept the nomination because of the great
need to fill the position.[20]

On October 11th, whether from sincere conviction
that it was outrageous to hire outsiders or from a desire to discredit Gibson, five councilmen publicly
criticized the Walker appointment and insisted there
should be no more like it.[21] President Turco at the
same time expressed his agreement with the councilmen
and denounced people who came to Newark "not to help
our residents but to establish for themselves a stepping stone to higher paying positions." Councilman
Harris, alluding to the fact that Walker's predecessor

Dr. Alan B. Clark had held the directorship for only
90 days, complained the "90-day hot-shots from out of
the state are using the city for a screening board to
other positions." He observed that not only Walker but
the Director of the Department of Finance and the Business Administrator had been brought to Newark from outside the state and warned the Mayor, "I hope you will
exercise great discretion before submitting any other
out-of-state nominees to us for confirmation--I will
not be in a receptive mood to confirm."[22]

Although the councilmen were exaggerating the situation, their criticisms were not without substance.
Mayor Gibson faced a dilemma in implementing his declared policy of recruiting the best qualified people
to head his government agencies. To go outside Newark
for highly skilled professionals meant running the risk
of appointing persons who would view their jobs as
steps on the way to higher professional positions.
Bailus Walker seems to have agreed with this analysis
when justifying his resignation in terms of his professional goals. He said, "all professionals hope to
move from the local to the state to the federal level
and eventually end up in some academic position." His
offer from the federal government had simply "developed
a little sooner than expected." Councilman James had
asserted that Walker's leaving was detrimental to the
city's health services, a point Walker denied; however,
when interviewed soon after arriving in Newark, Walker
had agreed that the previous uncertainty concerning
the department's leadership had been partly responsible
for the often reported weaknesses of the Newark health
services.[23]

## The Policemen React

From the standpoint of the success of the Washington nomination, the Walker resignation could not have
come at a worse moment. At the same time, the Ombudsman was dealt another heavy blow when, after remaining
silent about the ordinance, Newark's two policemen's

organizations launched an attack just before an appointment was to be made. As noted earlier, in 1965 the PBA
under the presidency of Anthony J. Giuliano had pick-
eted City Hall in opposition to a proposed civilian review board, and in 1968, Mayor Addonizio had proposed
an Ombudsman as an alternative to such a board, which
continued to be hotly opposed by Giuliano and the PBA.
In 1968, the PBA had shown no hostility towards the
idea of an Ombudsman, although in other American cities
(Buffalo, Oakland and Seattle) Ombudsman proposals had
been attacked by police spokesmen as civilian review
boards in disguise.

What is curious about events in Newark is that
police resistance materialized so late. There is no
record of anything having been said explicitly about
the Newark Ombudsman being a civilian police review
board at any of the Municipal Council meetings. Not
a word was reported publicly by any policemen until
after the private council meeting of October 3rd. The
first intimation of police opposition is to be found
in a newspaper account dated October 8th by Tex Novel-
lino, who covers City Hall for the *Star-Ledger*. After
mentioning that he had learned that Turco, Giuliano,
and Megaro were opposed to the Washington nomination,
he continued, "There is also expected to be some opposition from the Newark Police Department." Thus it
is clear that by the end of the first week of October,
the police had started on the warpath against the Ombudsman.

Why had they not set out earlier, and who initi-
ated the attack? Unfortunately, there are no certain
answers, but speculation suggests that one of two possible answers, or a combination of the two, seems likely. As was the case in Buffalo, an opponent of the
Ombudsman on the council may have drawn the attention
of the PBA to the threat of the new office, or the
President of the PBA may have taken action on his own
initiative. It is certainly not inconceivable that
Councilman Giuliano, a strong and persistent opponent
of the Ombudsman and President of the PBA at the time

it had successfully resisted civilian review boards,
urged current President Ronald Gasparinetti, to attack the Ombudsman as a last effort to prevent the
office from going into operation. Giuliano's influence on Gasparinetti's thinking, if not the timing of
his intervention, is suggested by the fact that one
of the two prongs of the latter's attack was that the
Ombudsman would be doing work that elected officials
such as the Mayor and Business Administrator should
be doing. This argument was presented by the councilman at the first and second readings of the ordinance and during the October 18th meeting on the nomination.

According to PBA President Gasparinetti, his attack on the Ombudsman was self-initiated and its timing was the result of his taking office as President
only on July 1st, after the passage of the ordinance.[24]
He described his predecessor Nicholas Gallichio (President, 1970-72) as ineffectual in protecting the interests of the union's members, and pointed to the failure
to oppose the Ombudsman ordinance as an example of such
delinquency. Gasparinetti believed that he had replaced
Gallichio because of the latter's failure to protect
union members and he perceived his role as president as
the protector of Newark policemen against all dangers,
actual, potential, or simply possible.

When interviewed by the writer, he revealed that
at some stage he had talked about the Ombudsman with
Gibson's Corporation Counsel William H. Walls, who had
told him that the last thing the Mayor had in mind was
for the Ombudsman to perform as a civilian police review board. Gasparinetti had retorted that it did not
matter what the Mayor's intention was so long as there
was a possibility that the Ombudsman might function as
a review board. In his public assault on the Ombudsman, Gasparinetti objected to the institution both because of its adverse effect on the police and on more
general grounds. When interviewed, he repeated the
general criticism but remarked that had the police been

exempt from the Ombudsman's jurisdiction, as head of
the PBA he would not have opposed the office. However,
with the police coming within the Ombudsman's scope,
he felt it necessary to take vigorous action to protect
his constituents.

There is some reason to believe that Gasparinetti's
hostility to the Ombudsman stemmed from personal exper-
iences as well as his role as the policeman's protector.
In 1968 he not only had campaigned for PBA office with
a "get tough" platform, but during the campaign the
Newark-Essex Chapter of CORE had asked for his dismis-
sal from the motorcycle squad because of unnecessarily
rough treatment of several members of the Black community.[25]

Gasparinetti's blast was released to the press on
October 10th, and appeared in the *Star-Ledger* the following day. Speaking as the representative of an organization that included a large majority of the Newark
police, he asked why there was a need for an Ombudsman
to do the work of the Mayor and Business Administrator.
His most serious charge, however, was that the Ombudsman was a civilian review board in disguise.

> As far as the police department is
> concerned, we are definitely opposed
> to the formation of an Ombudsman be-
> cause it would in fact be a civilian
> review board. A civilian review
> board is the worst possible thing
> that could happen to any city and its
> people.

A civilian review board meant that inexperienced and
inexpert laymen judge the work of experienced and expert policemen. Also, to subject the police to civilian review imposes still another threat to policemen,
who, Gasparinetti contended, were already deprived of
the constitutional immunity against self-incrimination
and double jeopardy that other citizens enjoyed.

Following on the heels of the PBA, the President
of the Newark Lodge 1 of the Fraternal Order of Police,
Newark's other smaller police union, on October 15th
issued his rebuff to the Ombudsman.[26] Interestingly,
no reference was made to the office as a kind of civilian review board. Instead, President James Brackin,
Jr., limited himself to a general, vaguely worded criticism, which suggests considerable ignorance of the
actual Ombudsman ordinance and seems to have been intended to play on the fears of city employees at the
expense of both the Mayor and the Municipal Council.
He chastised the Mayor and the council for increasing
the inefficiency of Newark government by adding more
"bosses, rules, and red tape." "The Mayor and the
Council are the ones who appointed the different heads
of the departments and now they can't run them. They
also blame some of their inefficiency on the city
workers." The Ombudsman was "a smokescreen to confuse
people" and was intended by the Mayor and the council
"to watch over and criticize everyone in the city but
themselves."

## Opposition by the Vailsburg Community Council

In addition to the two police unions a community
organization privately weighed in against the Ombudsman at this time with general arguments similar to
those of Gasparinetti and Brackin. These arguments
appeared in a letter sent to the Mayor on October 15th
by William Knapp, Jr., first vice president of the
Vailsburg Community Council. It seems probable that
the letter, declaring that the community council was
"definitely opposed to the idea of appointing a City
Ombudsman," was inspired by the police union's action.
The community council's letter may indicate some of
the pressures at this time on Michael P. Bottone, Councilman for the West Ward, which includes Vailsburg and
its predominantly white population. Bottone had voted
for the Ombudsman on three occasions in the spring.
The councilman, manager of a furniture company, des-

cribed himself when interviewed as mainly a business-
man and not a politician and boasted of his activities
on the council towards making Newark government more
efficient and frugal. Such a man might be expected to
be an Ombudsman supporter and it may be that his switch
in November was the result of constituency pressures
such as that of the Vailsburg Community Council of
which he is a member. On the other hand, it is conceivable that Bottone himself inspired the Vailsburg
letter.

## Dwindling Council Support

It is doubtful whether even in the absence of the
"outsider" issue and the opposition of the police u-
nions, the Washington nomination would have won the
five votes needed to pass the Municipal Council. What
is more certain is that the two events sealed the des-
truction of the Ombudsman. Councilmen Harris and
James had for months fulminated against "carpetbaggers"
and the Bailus Walker resignation was bound to have ex-
acerbated their feelings on the subject. Indeed, Harris's notice to Gibson on October 11th had amounted to
a warning that he would vote against Washington. Since
Anthony J. Giuliano was a firm opponent of the Ombudsman from the beginning, police opposition could have
had no effect on his vote; however, it may have influenced Michael Bontempo, who had spent nearly a quarter
of a century on the Newark police force before becoming Councilman-at-Large in 1954. Bontempo supported
the Ombudsman in May in council debate and by voting
for the April resolution and the first and second readings, but he opposed the institution in October.

Robert Washington was interviewed by the council
on October 17th and seems to have impressed just about
every member; however, by this stage it seems clear
that no matter how impressive Washington's bearing and
qualifications could have been, the majority of councilmen were determined not to have him as Ombudsman.
On October 18th, the council rejected the nomination
by a vote of six to two with one abstention.[27]

## Conflict on Other Issues the Day the Ombudsman Was Defeated

Like most minutes, those of the Newark Municipal Council are sparse and largely formal, but a reading of the council minutes for October 18th reveals abundant evidence of the intense conflict between Mayor Gibson and most of the councilmen. It was an especially bad day for the Mayor, with the defeat of the Ombudsman being the last and greatest blow dealt his administration by the council. Citizens' complaints to the council about the lack of or poor quality of city services allowed the councilmen to play the role of defenders of the public against the inefficiency of the Mayor's administration, and to reiterate their position that federal funds should be devoted to getting such services to the public.

Shortly after this discussion of the need to spend "federal dollars" on essential services such as sewerage, garbage collection, and tree trimming, the council by a vote of seven to one returned to Mayor Gibson unapproved a resolution authorizing him to expand the Public Employment Program to provide employment training for up to 640 Newark residents.[28] The council meeting had begun about 8 P.M. About 10 P.M., the question of the use of federal funds again came up when Sharpe James moved that President Turco appoint "a 'watchdog' committee to oversee the City's expenditures of funds received for implementation of Federal programs." The motion also required that "copies of any audits and/or evaluation reports of the aforesaid Federal funds be submitted forthwith by the Administration to the Municipal Council." Turco himself seconded the motion, and after it was passed with the support of eight councilmen (Westbrooks abstaining), he proceeded to appoint James to chair the new committee. A better example of the cooperation of Black and white councilmen in their struggle with the Mayor would be difficult to find, unless it be the action taken a few minutes later when the Washington nomination was rejected.

## VOTING AGAINST THE OFFICE

The motion to confirm the nomination of Robert Washington was made by Dennis Westbrooks, but instead of Earl Harris seconding the motion as had happened during the two readings of the ordinance, Louis Turco was the seconder. Turco explained that while he still did not think an Ombudsman was needed in Newark and believed that the office would duplicate existing services, he nevertheless would vote for Washington because he had been so impressed by the nominee's ability and thought he would be an asset to the city. This strange reasoning is no more bizarre than Turco's total voting record on the Ombudsman issue. He managed to take every possible position, abstaining during the vote on the first reading of the ordinance, voting against the second reading, and voting for the Ombudsman at the nomination stage. Such a voting pattern strongly suggests an effort to avoid responsibility for accepting or rejecting the Ombudsman. The certainty of Washington's defeat on October 18th allowed him to vote for the Mayor's candidate.

That most of the council on this occasion were voting against the office of Ombudsman and not the person nominated to fill it is suggested by the arguments recorded in the minutes. Only Earl Harris stated that the character of the nominee influenced his adverse vote. A rigid opponent of non-resident city appointments, he vowed to vote against any person who was not a resident of Newark. Most of the remarks made by the councilman were aimed at the ordinance. Sharpe James praised Robert Washington as a "talented individual" but maintained that he was "being recommended for the wrong position at the wrong time." The argument most frequently used against the office was that it would be a duplication of the services of existing complaint handling organizations.[29] Councilman James summed up this position when he exclaimed, "The last thing citizens need is another complaint mechanism." In the minds of councilmen, this argument is closely linked to the slightly different one that it

is up to the Mayor to keep his officials from abusing
authority.[30]  A third argument employed on this occa-
tion was that public funds should be spent not on complaint handling but on providing regular local services,
which were currently inadequate in Newark.[31]

Only Dennis Westbrooks spoke in favor of the Ombudsman.  He reminded the council it had discussed and
approved the office several months before.  "The position was established and now the position is being
filled."  However, realizing that not only the nomination but also the office itself was at stake, he proceeded to rebut arguments against the latter.  Councilmen opposing the Ombudsman had emphasized the need to
deliver city government services to the people, but,
in Westbrooks's view, the Ombudsman himself would provide an important service.  Rather than duplicate, the
new office would complement the activities and achievements of Action Now, which had neither the resources
nor authority of an Ombudsman.  Westbrooks's reasoning
fell on deaf ears.

*Summary of opposition arguments*.  Briefly, councilmen's arguments against Newark's having an Ombudsman focused on two points.  First:  the office would
duplicate work that should be done by existing government agencies.  Stated by Giuliano on May 3rd, the
point was repeated during the two subsequent public
meetings when the council considered the Ombudsman.
Second:  federal money coming to Newark should be
spent only on regular basic public services such as
police, sewerage, and garbage collecting.  This argument was offered only at the October 18th meeting.

It is impossible to be certain whether the councilmen actually believed these contentions, but there
is some reason to conclude that they did in fact find
them convincing.  In addition, Business Administrator
Bodine expressed to the writer his agreement with the
latter argument.  Thus it appears that many of the
people participating in the decision on a Newark Ombudsman never understood the difference between that
office and Action Now.

## Councilmen's Fears

Did councilmen have reasons for opposing the Ombudsman in addition to those noted above? The opposition of the PBA was undoubtedly in the minds of some councilmen on October 18th. Also, some of them may have been disturbed by the belief that the Ombudsman would be the Mayor's pawn. When interviewed by the writer, Dennis Westbrooks said that several councilmen were concerned for this reason, and in their interviews both Michael Bottone and Sharpe James expressed such fears. In view of Newark's political traditions, it is perhaps not surprising that councilmen should be suspicious that an office holder picked by the Mayor would be used to his political advantage and possibly their disadvantage.

Two additional elements may have played a part in their thinking. It seems likely that the vote against the Washington nomination was in part an expression of the general hostility several councilmen felt towards the Mayor; or, at least, that councilmen were inhibited by no bonds of personal or political friendship from frustrating his Ombudsman plans, and some undoubtedly found pleasure in thwarting the Mayor. Finally, one cannot rule out the possibility that some of the pre-1970 councilmen, who had profited from the corruption of Newark politics, were not happy with the idea of an investigating agency that might unearth dubious governmental practices.

## The Mayor's Reaction to Defeat

The day following the rejection of his candidate, Kenneth Gibson issued a statement to the press announcing that the council left him no alternative but to return to the federal government the $261,900 that OEO had provided for the Ombudsman. "The City Council," he explained, "could not conceivably have been saying no to Mr. Washington; they were saying no to the concept of the Ombudsman."[32] The rejection of the Ombuds-

man, he characteristically argued, was not a defeat for
his administration, for "the only defeat the Gibson administration could have had was if we did not recognize
the need for one." The Municipal Council was excoriated
for "denying the people of Newark a man who would be
capable of ridding the City Government of many of the
malpractices that we all know exist."

The Mayor appealed to the people "to recognize how
severely the action of the City Council would affect
the future of this city." Newark was in "dire need" of
financial assistance, yet the council had obliged the
Mayor "for the flimsiest reasons" to return money to
the federal government. The public was also reminded
of the cost to Newark taxpayers for the time and effort
of the Mayor's office in planning for the Ombudsman.
The irresponsible way in which the council had first
approved the Ombudsman and then turned around and ve-
toed their own action would, Gibson warned, "cause Washington to think twice before approving any programs for
the City of Newark." Curiously, in view of his attack
on the council, the Mayor's statement concluded by saying, "I do not consider this a fight with the City Council. I consider this a fight of the old against the
new."

Kenneth Gibson's decision not to make further efforts to implement the Ombudsman ordinance after the
council action of October 18th appears to have resulted
from his conviction that nothing he could do would bring
the council to allow the Ombudsman's office to begin operations under a properly qualified person. When interviewed by the writer on November 2, 1972, he was asked
whether he would consider nominating another candidate.
His answer was an emphatic "no." He had put before the
council the best qualified person he could find and the
council had rejected him. He was not now going to let
the council make the appointment.

When asked why he did not follow the practice of
the President of the United States, who makes a second
nomination after the Senate refuses his first choice,

the Mayor replied that the Senate gives reasons for its rejection. Reminded that the council also gave reasons, Gibson retorted that they were not good reasons and added that whoever he nominated would be unacceptable to the council, which did not want an Ombudsman.

## HOPE, AND THE OEO POSITION

Not everyone favoring a Newark Ombudsman was as prepared as the Mayor to accept the finality of the October 18th defeat. When interviewed on November 2nd, Councilman Westbrooks expressed his belief that the Mayor should nominate another candidate, as there was some chance that a majority of the council might support him.

In Washington, Ira Kaye of OEO continued into December to hope that something still might be done to get the Newark Ombudsman into operation. Early in November, he wrote to the Mayor's office saying how distressed he was by the council's action, which had caused difficulties not only for Newark but also for his own office, and to the Ombudsman Activities Project. OEO was in the embarrassing position of having made a major commitment to Newark in time and money only to find itself halfway through the grant period without an Ombudsman. OAP had also spent time and money on the Newark project and had been obliged to hold in continuing abeyance the planning and work assignments for technical assistance and evaluation elsewhere. Because of these difficulties, Kaye gave the Mayor and the council a deadline of December 15th for filling the Ombudsman's office. If no appointment were made by that date, OEO would have to take steps to recover the grant. December 15th came and went with no appointment, and the last breath went out of the Newark Ombudsman.

## Why an Ombudsman Was Not
## Established in Newark

THREE VIEWS

This monograph has revealed a number of factors contributing to the failure of plans for an Ombudsman in Newark. Before summarizing and assessing their importance, it would be well to mention the views of some of the principal participants, who have expressed opinions to the writer. In fairness to these three persons, it should be emphasized that the opinions expressed are not necessarily their full thinking on the subject.

When interviewed, Mayor Gibson attributed the rejection of the Ombudsman and the Washington appointment to three circumstances: (1) the opposition of the PBA; (2) the fact that some councilmen were supporting other candidates; and (3) the desire of some councilmen simply to oppose the Mayor. Gibson did not say whether he believed any one circumstance was more important than the others, nor did he mention several factors to which this report has attributed significance.[1]

When Dennis Westbrooks was asked to explain the defeat of the Washington nomination, he did so by attributing various councilmen's votes to different single factors. Earl Harris had voted against Washington because he was a non-resident, while Sharpe James was motivated by personal hostility towards the Mayor. Anthony Giuliano and Michael Bontempo were influenced by the opposition of the PBA. Bontempo was described by Westbrooks as a retired policeman who would consequently be inclined

to go along with the PBA position, and Giuliano as being
on a leave of absence from the police, a circumstance
that obliged him to support the PBA in order to protect
his career. Ralph Villani always went along with the
majority of white councilmen. Louis Turco had voted
for Washington after voting against the ordinance so as
to have it both ways and therefore not offend anyone.

Westbrooks did not say whether the factors he mentioned were the only ones affecting the voting of the
respective councilmen or simply the most important ones.
First, his explanation would clearly be unsatisfactory,
since it is highly unlikely that in all of the cases
mentioned a single circumstance caused the voting. Second, the explanation is unsatisfactory since it failed
to specify the other circumstances that had to be present for the factor mentioned to cause a vote against
Washington. However, earlier in the interview, Westbrooks did suggest one such circumstance: that the May-
or shared the blame for the Ombudsman failure because
he did not make any effort to work with the council.
On the other hand, Westbrooks's analysis is a useful re-
minder that the explanation of votes by one anti-Ombuds-
man councilman is not necessarily the same as that for
the others. His explanation concerning Councilman Villani is especially interesting in this respect and probably correct. An important figure in Newark politics
in the past, Villani was 71 by the time the Ombudsman
came before the Municipal Council. He had become severely disabled by illness and was unable to speak.[2]
Had Bontempo and Bottone joined Turco in voting for
Washington, in Westbrooks's view there would have been
a strong likelihood of Villani also coming along.

Patricia Stolfa, the OEO official most involved in
trying to implant an Ombudsman in Newark, perceived the
defeat of the Ombudsman differently from both Gibson and
Westbrooks and stressed not the motivation of councilmen
but certain characteristics of Newark society. The initiative for instituting an Ombudsman had been taken not
by a broadly based movement in Newark but by officials in
OEO. "Newark did not come to us with a bunch of people

who thought they ought to have an Om[budsman].  We told
them that was what we could give them and they took it
and did what they could with it."  As a result, there
was no "constituency" in Newark favoring the institution.  The Ombudsman was "not reflective of what people
in the Community want and can see as a solution to their
most pressing problems."

Besides this lack of grass-roots support, Stolfa
described as a second factor

> the political climate in Newark...
> is such that the rather conservative
> reform style of an Om[budsman] was
> neither acceptable nor beneficial.
> Things are just too wild and woolly
> there.  Politics is an ugly and
> dirty business, and the lack of a
> real community that had some faith
> in government was critical.[3]

Stolfa stressed two significant aspects of the Ombudsman's
failure mentioned neither by Gibson nor Westbrooks--the
absence of very strong commitment by the Mayor and of influential groups of Newark citizens publicly supporting
the reform.  She is incorrect, however, in her apparent
belief that no influential groups favoring the Ombudsman
idea existed in Newark.  The mystery is why they were not
active in 1972.

## FACTORS IN THE FAILURE:
## A DISCUSSION

Informational gaps and uncertainty make it impossible to provide a totally adequate explanation for the
failure to establish a Newark Ombudsman.  What can be
said with assurance is that several factors were involved
in the failure, some more influential than others.  These
factors are described below along with attempts to assess
their influence.

## Legal Framework

*The Newark Ombudsman would have gone into operation had it not been for the legal framework in which the policy was evolved.* The Mayor's office concluded that it was legally obliged to take the Ombudsman proposal through the Municipal Council; that given that obligation it was best to create the office by ordinance. The ordinance itself then required that the council agree to the appointment of someone to fill the office.

OEO officials were aware of the problem of council hostility and urged Gibson to bypass the council in creating the new office. On the other hand, it does not appear to have occurred to the same officials to advise avoiding the council altogether, including the appointment of a person to fill the new office. Here the influence of the Gellhorn Model Statute, which OEO was determined should be followed as closely as possible, seems to have blinded officials to the idea of setting up an executive Ombudsman in Newark, at least to begin with.

Whatever OEO might have advised or allowed, the legal requirement would still have remained to involve the council at the establishment stage, and it is quite possible--indeed probable--that the council would have conditioned its acceptance of the Ombudsman upon being given a part in filling the office. Had there been no legal need to seek council acceptance of the Ombudsman, undoubtedly the office would have gone into operation. The requirement of council agreement, however, in itself did not destroy the Ombudsman, for if other factors had not been present, the council would have gone along with the Mayor.

## Level of Mayor's Commitment

*Because the Mayor was only moderately committed to the Ombudsman policy, his struggle was not as effective as if he had perceived it as a matter of prime importance.*

58

To point out this lack of high commitment is in no sense a criticism of a mayor contending with urban problems on Newark's level. Indeed, it can be argued that it would have been reprehensible for Kenneth Gibson to make a great effort for the success of the Ombudsman at the expense of settling more important issues. As Philip Douglas observed,

> The Ombudsman idea was not considered so vital that Gibson would flex any unusual amount of political muscle to counteract the shadow forces opposing it. What little muscle an honest mayor has in Newark is usually reserved for more critical battles.[4]

Still, the facts remain that the extra effort was not made and that the Newark Ombudsman proposal was without such highly committed champions as were available for similar proposals in Hawaii and Nebraska, where respectively State Senators Duke Kawasaki and Loran Schmit personally waged vigorous campaigns for their proposals. The outcome of the Newark effort might have been different if there had not been other more important issues to divert Gibson's attention, or if he had perceived the Ombudsman as worthy of a greater expenditure of political capital, or had the Newark Municipal Council contained an influential member with the commitment of a Kawasaki or a Schmit.


## Mayor-Council Conflict

*Conflict between Mayor Gibson and the Municipal Council greatly diminished the likelihood that the council would accept the Ombudsman.* Kenneth Gibson would have encountered far fewer difficulties with the council about the Ombudsman had his relations with councilmen been generally harmonious. In fact, the opposite was the case for several reasons, including (1) the absence of a city party organization led by

the Mayor and including a majority of councilmen (a
circumstance much influenced by Newark's non-partisan
electoral system); (2) the continual efforts of councilmen to broaden their governmental role; (3) Gibson's
resistance to these efforts; (4) his unconcealed reformer's disdain for councilmen, perceived by him as
holdovers from Newark's corrupt and inefficient past;
and (5) councilmen's perception of the Mayor as a competitor for electoral support.

While it is likely that the Municipal Council
would have accepted the Ombudsman had its relations
with the Mayor generally been close and cordial, it
does not follow that poor Mayor-council relations
alone account for the Ombudsman's defeat. It must
be remembered that the council has passed a number
of Gibson's proposals, often only after considerable
struggle sometimes concluded by compromises agreeable
to both sides.

Also, while relations between Gibson and the council are poor, they are worse on some occasions than
others, a fact of which the Mayor was abundantly aware
when he delayed submitting the Ombudsman ordinance in
February 1972. After the Planned Variations compromises, Mayor-council relations improved and the council did act positively towards the Ombudsman in April
and May. These considerations lead to a third factor
contributing to the Ombudsman's defeat.

## Awkward Timing

*The timing of the recruitment activities preceding
establishment of the Ombudsman diminished the chances
of the office going into operation.* Because relations
between the Mayor and council fluctuated during the
period the Ombudsman was being promoted, it was important that the office come before the council during a
period of improved relations and, more generally, when
there were a minimum of external pressures on councilmen to oppose it. As indicated above, through February

and March Gibson postponed submitting the ordinance, which was in proper form by the end of January. Ironically, this timing decision appears to have influenced two other decisions by the Mayor, which may have had a detrimental effect on the success of the Ombudsman. Because the nominee, Earl Phillips, seemed especially well qualified for the job and because the Mayor was uncertain whether the Ombudsman ordinance would ever be passed, Phillips was appointed instead to be director of a new anti-crime program. This decision both removed a candidate who could not possibly be described as a non-resident, and presented the Mayor with the problem of finding a new candidate. At this point, he took a fateful decision and postponed the search until the ordinance was passed. Given the possibilities that the council might not accept the ordinance or that several months might pass before they did, one can understand why the Mayor took the decision. Its consequences, however, may have been fatal for the Ombudsman. Only after the ordinance passed its first reading on May 17th did the search for a new Ombudsman nominee begin, and Robert B. Washington was not chosen by the Mayor until August. When the nomination finally got before the council on September 20th, Mayor-council relations had again taken a turn for the worse.

Had Mayor Gibson nominated Earl Phillips for Ombudsman in late May or early June instead of Robert Washington in late September, there are several reasons for thinking that there would have been a much greater likelihood of the nomination being accepted: (1) Mayor-council relations were better in May than in late September. (2) The council, having just accepted the ordinance, would have found it much more embarrassing to oppose it three or four days rather than four months later. (3) Ronald Gasparinetti did not become President of the PBA until July 1972 and consequently it is likely that PBA opposition would not have occurred in May or June.

## Foresight and Luck

(4) As noted earlier, Earl Phillips could not have been depicted as a non-resident in the same way as Robert Washington was to be.

The foregoing reason is not a matter of timing and, since it could have been foreseen by the Mayor's office, cannot be termed fortuitous. In addition, the effects of postponing filling the Ombudsman's office also could have been predicted and they too are not fortuitous. However, it would have been next to impossible for the Mayor and his staff to predict the course of Mayor-council relations, and one could hardly expect them to have been aware in May of the change which was to take place in July in the PBA. In the sense that these last two events could not have been foreseen by the Mayor's office, one can say that the failure of the Ombudsman can in part be attributed to bad luck.

## Lack of Mass Support

*The rejection of the Ombudsman was less harmful politically to the councilmen than the rejection of certain other types of proposals from the Mayor.* The Mayor made no effort until the last minute to attract popular support, and the lone newspaper editorial which resulted was too little and too late to help the Ombudsman. It is doubtful, however, whether a greater effort would have appreciably improved his chances. Experience of the adoption of Ombudsmen abroad and in this country indicates that an Ombudsman policy, like other policies involving administrative reform and civil liberties, is highly unlikely to elicit strong popular support. As Stanley Anderson has aptly understated it, "The office is not likely to be swept into being by grassroots clamor."[5] This means that it would have been difficult for the Mayor's office to drum up popular support to counteract the opposition of councilmen.

## Lack of Interest Group Support

*There was a total absence of interest group activity on behalf of Mayor Gibson's proposed Ombudsman, which relieved councilmen of the need to take into consideration the views of such groups.* If there is no reason to expect an Ombudsman policy to receive broad popular support, experience shows that certain kinds of interest groups often actively promote such policies. The absence of such support in Newark is especially odd in light of the success of the organizers of the 1969-70 *ad hoc* New Jersey Ombudsman Committee. They brought together 23 New Jersey organizations to sponsor and finance the May 25, 1970, Ombudsman Conference in Newark. Among the organizations lending support at that time were the Greater Newark Urban Coalition, the Greater Newark Chamber of Commerce, the Newark Jaycees, the New Jersey State Bar Association, the New Jersey State AFL-CIO, and the New Jersey Council of Churches.

If such an impressive coalition of sectional and promotional interest groups, which were sympathetic towards the Ombudsman idea in 1970, had publicly supported the Gibson proposal in 1972, undoubtedly that proposal's chances of success would have improved. In fact, neither those who organized the 1970 conference nor a single representative of the organizations sponsoring it appeared before the Municipal Council to argue on behalf of the Ombudsman (a situation that differs significantly from that in Seattle in 1969-70 when that city's Ombudsman was being established.)[6] Neither did any of these individuals or organizations issue any public statements supporting the Mayor's Ombudsman proposal. According to Edwin F. Melick, chairman of the 1970 Ombudsman Conference, his group of Ombudsman advocates, which had dwindled considerably in numbers since 1970, had been concentrating on promoting a state Ombudsman while the Mayor's office was trying to establish the Newark Ombudsman. Joel R. Jacobson, the most active New Jersey labor union supporter of Ombudsmen, lent no assistance to the Newark Ombudsman be-

cause he was generally disappointed with Gibson's performance and did not have very good relations with him.[7]

For its part, the Mayor's office did nothing to
enlist civic group support for its Ombudsman policy.
This neglect was partly the result of the inexperience
of the Mayor's aides who were left to handle such matters. Norman Abrams admits that he was new to the job
of policy promotion in 1972 and that the thought of
mobilizing the support of "good government" groups had
not occurred to him. In fact, Abrams had never heard
of the *ad hoc* Committee on the Ombudsman or of the 1970
Ombudsman Conference.

But inexperience, he believes, is only part of the
reason for the failure to mobilize civic groups.

> I never thought of it because I
> had never seen them used in other
> matters and no one thought their
> possible contribution significant
> enough to ever suggest it as a
> possible resource to me....I was
> not so new that I did not think
> to ask everyone I met for advice
> every step of the way.[8]

Since the 1950's, "good government" groups in Newark
have been so inactive in city politics that today they
rarely think of themselves or are thought of by others
as significant influences on policymaking. Even had
they attempted to influence the Ombudsman decisions of
the Municipal Council, given the political attitudes
and style of councilmen, civic group views probably
would not have had very much impact. The most one can
say is that a civic group campaign would have made at
least a small contribution toward the Ombudsman's success.

Failure to Involve Councilmen

*Neither the Mayor's office nor the Ombudsman Activities Project made any significant effort to explain the character and advantages of the Ombudsman to the Municipal Council, or to involve councilmen in the establishment of the office.* With three exceptions, the Mayor's office seems not to have tried to directly influence councilmen's thinking. The efforts included: Business Administrator Bodine's short memorandum when the ordinance was sent to the council, his meeting with the council on April 18th to discuss acceptance of the OEO grant; and Mayor Gibson's last minute meeting with the council on October 3rd. At no other time does it appear that the Mayor or his staff met with councilmen collectively or individually to discuss the Ombudsman project. In this connection, scholars in the Ombudsman Activities Project might have been called in to talk with councilmen and to allay some of their fears, but the Mayor's office did not request such assistance, and Stanley Anderson, the Project Director, who was sensitive about his organization becoming involved at this stage, did not offer such help. Anderson's diffidence is understandable in light of attitudes within the Mayor's office. During one of her visits to Newark, Patricia Stolfa offered assistance in explaining the Ombudsman proposal to councilmen and others. The offer was turned down on the ground that the Mayor's office would get the proposal through the council not by explaining its merits but by political bargaining.[9]

The neglect of councilmen at the recruitment stage was particularly unfortunate. The Mayor and his aides undoubtedly reasoned, probably correctly, that any candidates proposed by the council would not have been qualified for the position. Yet councilmen could have been involved in ways that could have prevented this from happening. In the case of the Seattle/King County Ombudsman, the legislation establishing the office provided for a Citizens' Advisory Commission, appointed

by the Seattle and King County councils, to submit a
list of at least five names for Ombudsman to the councils, which would make the final selection.[10] Some
variation on this device along with informal mayoral
consultation might have influenced some Newark councilmen to go along with a qualified appointee.

It probably would be incorrect to assign much
weight to these factors in an explanation of the Ombudsman's failure, for council opposition stemmed from
more than misunderstanding and lack of involvement.
Such efforts would only have marginally improved the
Ombudsman's chances; but, along with other actions,
they might have tilted the council balance in the office's favor.

## The "Carpetbagger" Issue

*From the standpoint of his acceptability to the
council, Robert Washington was a poor choice. He was
perceived by several councilmen as a "carpetbagger" at
a time when, because of the Bailus Walker resignation,
resentment against appointment of outsiders was especially strong.* The Mayor's nomination of Washington
was in line with his policy of appointing to city offices the best qualified persons he could find, regard-
less of residence. The fact that Washington had not
lived in Newark for several years gave councilmen another excuse for voting against the nomination. In the
case of Earl Harris, it was probably an important influence on his vote.

## PBA Opposition

*The last minute opposition of the PBA added to the
difficulty of getting the Ombudsman through the council.* It is hard to estimate with any precision the
strength of this factor. The fate of the Ombudsman
was much in doubt at least a week before the PBA's
attack on October 10th. Given Mayor Gibson's uncom-

promising stand on the Washington nomination and the decision by a number of councilmen on October 3rd to question the very existence of the newly created Ombudsman office, it is doubtful whether the Ombudsman would have survived, even in the absence of the PBA intervention. It thus remains uncertain whether Ronald Gasparinetti finished off the Ombudsman or merely slammed the lid on his coffin.

## Lack of a Second Nomination

*By refusing to put forward another candidate after Washington's defeat, the Mayor precluded any possibility of saving the Ombudsman by nominating another person capable of filling the office but acceptable to a majority of the council.* Whether Gibson's inaction was a major factor or none at all in the failure of the Ombudsman depends on information that, unfortunately, this monograph is unable to provide with any certainty. Could the Mayor have found a candidate who would have satisfactorily filled the role of a classical Ombudsman and at the same time received the votes of five councilmen in October or November 1972? To answer in the affirmative one would have to know, first, that there were at least five councilmen who were prepared to accept a qualified candidate, and, second, that after the defeat of Washington there was still a qualified candidate available.

Kenneth Gibson did not believe that either of these conditions prevailed. He seems to have thought that in turning down Washington the council was defeating the office and that, even if this were not the case, councilmen would never accept a qualified candidate. When Norman Abrams and Marvin McGraw, the two aides who handled the Ombudsman policy, were later asked if something could not have been done to find a candidate acceptable to both Mayor and council, both interpreted the council's action on October 18th as expressing determination to kill an institution they perceived as a threat to themselves.[11] Abrams also believed, however, that an unqualified candidate well known to councilmen might have been found acceptable.

On the other hand, when interviewed shortly after the October 18th meeting, Councilman Westbrooks was of the opinion that a compromise candidate, presumably qualified, might still get through the council, and it was possible that Gibson and his aides were overly pessimistic. Such a compromise candidate, if he had agreed to be nominated, would have been Roger Lowenstein. After the rejection of Robert Washington, Gibson appears to have made a mistake in judgment in not nominating Lowenstein or someone with similar qualifications.

## CONCLUSION

If the office of Newark Ombudsman had gone into operation, it would have proven an interesting and useful experiment with that institution in a city exhibiting in extreme form most of the problems of contemporary urban life. Quite possibly the experiment would have failed. This is the view of Philip Douglas:

> In retrospect an Ombudsman probably
> would not have succeeded in Newark.
> The city is so polarized, the polit-
> ical forces so diverse and mobilized,
> the bureaucracy so unresponsive, and
> the economic conditions so extreme,
> that an independent investigator of
> citizen complaints backed by no polit-
> ical force of his own, would have been
> eaten alive in a matter of months.[12]

If this had happened, it would have been a strong argument against classical Ombudsmen, and for executive Ombudsmen--dependent on and deriving influence from the Mayor--in cities like Newark. As it is, the social experiment remains unperformed. It is difficult not to conclude that more could have been done by the Ombudsman's proponents to get the office established. Whether or not greater efforts to line up the support of councilmen and to mobilize civic groups behind the reform would have overcome the obstacles to success is impossible to judge with any certainty, but with a little bit of luck they just might have made it.

The nature of the Ombudsman institution should make it relatively easy to establish. Compared to other public organizational innovations, an Ombudsman is inexpensive, unlikely to disrupt the operations of existing organization, and equally unlikely to do so if, after an unsuccessful trial, it is abolished. Despite numerous proposals for Ombudsmen at all levels of American government, however, very few have been established. When compared to successful efforts elsewhere, the failure of the effort in Newark to create an Ombudsman does suggest certain conditions that should be present if a mayor is to promote the institution successfully.

Although operative Ombudsmen have caused little discontent among persons affected by them, in Newark and elsewhere Ombudsmen proposals have led to fear and consequent opposition from legislators and administrators. To counteract this opposition, a mayor attempting to establish an Ombudsman may have to adopt the following means: (1) Allay the fears of legislators and administrators through an intensive and persuasive explanation of the character of an Ombudsman; (2) mobilize civic groups on behalf of the institution; (3) use his prestige and good will among legislators to enlist their support. In Newark, for reasons discussed above, none of these means was employed and the proposed Ombudsman never went into operation.

On the other hand, it has also been seen that whatever political skills Mayor Gibson and his aides might have used, conditions of Newark politics were such that their success would have been uncertain. In a city like Newark, a reforming mayor is not likely to get along with a city council composed mainly of traditional urban

American politicians for whom logrolling, patronage, favoritism, and conflicts-of-interest are all part of the job. In this circumstance, it is unwise for a mayor--at least to begin with--to try to establish a classical Ombudsman dependent on creation and appointment by the city council. An executive Ombudsman, over whom the council has no control, would seem more likely to succeed.[13] The experience of the Iowa Citizens' Aide Office indicates that if the chief executive is willing, an executive Ombudsman can exhibit most of the characteristics and benefits of a classical Ombudsman. As in Iowa after two years, if political conditions should become favorable in time, an executive Ombudsman can be transformed by legislation into a full-fledged classical one. Should such conditions not occur, an executive Ombudsman modeled on classical lines would be better than no Ombudsman at all.

For cities not dominated by traditional urban politicians, the prospects of appointing a classical Ombudsman at the outset seem much more encouraging. In this circumstance, the education of councilmen and administrators not to fear an Ombudsman and the mobilization of civic groups in support of the innovation would be more easily accomplished, while relations between the city council and the reforming mayor would probably be more amiable. Once in operation, a classical Ombudsman would have a considerably better chance for success in such a setting than it would have in a political environment such as Newark's.

# NOTES TO CHAPTER I

[1] Ron Porambo, *No Cause for Indictment* (New York: Holt, Rinehart and Winston, 1971), pp. 44-45; Governor's Select Commission on Civil Disorder, State of New Jersey, *Report for Action* (February 1968), pp. 11, 36.

[2] *Report for Action* p. 164.

[3] The idea of a Newark Ombudsman was not new to Addonizio. Joel R. Jacobson, President of the New Jersey Industrial Council, AFL-CIO, said he had suggested an Ombudsman to Addonizio in 1965. Throughout the second half of the 1960's Jacobson was a vocal supporter for an Ombudsman both in Newark and at the state level.

[4] Newark *Sunday Star-Ledger*, April 28, 1968. Section 1, p. 6. The OEO offer seems to have been made on March 6th, according to a report in the Newark *Evening News,* the next day.

[5] Norman N. Schiff, "Creation of the Municipal Ombudsman." The unpublished report includes 22 pages of discussion and an eight page draft statute. For the Gellhorn statute, see Stanley V. Anderson (ed.), *Ombudsmen for American Government?* (Englewood Cliffs: Prentice-Hall, 1968), Appendix.

[6] *Summary Report of the New Jersey Conference on the Ombudsman,* n.d. In the following December, as noted in the newspapers on December 21, 1970, the steering committee of the New Jersey Committee recommended the creation of a state Ombudsman, mentioning also the possibility of expanding the office "to provide citizens with a method of redressing grievances relating to matters handled by county and local governments." *Summary Report,* p. 19. At that time, the *Summary Report* was sent to the Governor, members of the state

Notes to Chapter I cont'd

legislature, and state Supreme Court Justices. Senate
Bill 34, introduced by Raymond Bateman, had passed the
State Senate on May 11, 1972, but by mid-March 1973
was bottled up in the Assembly Committee on State Government.

[7] *Report for Action*, p. 17.

[8] *Newark Human Rights Commission: 1952-1972*
(Newark: Newark Public Information Office, 1972),
pp. 5-6. *Information: A Paper for the People of
Newark* (August 21, 1972), p. 10. In 1972, the commission had an annual budget of $200,000. It is
housed in the basement of City Hall and the present
Executive Director is Daniel W. Blue, Jr., a Black
detective on leave from the police force.

[9] Newark *Evening News*, June 12, 1968, p. 23.

[10] "The First Twelve Months: A Look at the Past,
a Strategy for the Future," a speech by Mayor Gibson
at the end of his first year in office, July 1, 1971.
A leaflet circulated by Action Now urged people to
come to it with problems about city government agencies, employers, landlords, and merchants or salesmen.
Examples of Action Now cases are provided in some edi-
tions of *Information*. Gibson appointed a Black executive director of Action Now, Rev. Ralph T. Grant.

[11] *Action Now Annual Report*, 1971-72. See Appendix I for an overview of Action Now's first year's
work.

[12] Interview with Joseph Bradley, November 2, 1972.
If the councilmen's information is correct, it could,
of course, be interpreted as showing the success of
Action Now in stimulating people with complaints to
seek remedies.

Notes to Chapter I cont'd

13 Interviewed November 1, 1972.

14 While there is no evidence that Mayor Gibson
controls the day-to-day activities of Action Now, a
leaflet circulated in Newark to publicize the organization suggests that he is not adverse to using it to
brighten his political image. The leaflet contains a
picture of Mayor Gibson accompanied by a short letter
from him to "Dear Fellow Newarker" in which he states,
"No longer will the 'red tape' of City Hall stand in
the way of getting your results fast. I understand
your frustration and am doing something about it." A
picture of Gibson also appears prominently on the
first page of the first annual report of Action Now,
followed by a page emphasizing that the organization
shows that the Mayor had made good on his campaign
promise to deliver city services to the people as
quickly as possible. The report also proclaims on
page 2: "Mayor Gibson, in his efforts to lead a city
like Newark successfully, needs the support of everyone if he is to succeed."

15 They included the failure of the city to prune
trees despite several requests; and a retired city official's complaint that he and others in a similar position were not being treated the same as other officials with respect to retirement benefits. According
to *Information*, types of complaints differ according
to the character of the ward.

16 Wilcox, "Origins of an Ombudsman Office," pp. 11-
12. Wilcox's account appears as Appendix I of John E.
Moore, *The Joint Seattle/King County Office of Citizen
Complaints: An Interim Analysis and Evaluation for
the Period May 1971 through June 1972* (Report...to OEO,
December 31, 1972).

Notes to Chapter I cont'd

[17] Besides reading Gellhorn's books, Wilcox traveled to New York City to discuss the OEO projects with him. In spite of his great influence on OEO's Ombudsman projects, this appears to have been Professor Gellhorn's only personal contact with OEO, and he has only a vague memory of that occasion. (Letter from Walter Gellhorn to the writer, February 21, 1973.) In their discussions of Ombudsman projects, OEO officials considered sponsoring a variety of Ombudsmen, some along classical Gellhorn lines and some not. Whatever their intention, funding in fact supported only classical Ombudsmen. In addition to complaints against government officials, the OEO at this time was also interested in consumers' complaints. Among other things, it pumped money into Newark's Consumer Affairs Project with the result that the agency, which began in 1970 with a staff of three, had a staff of 20 by the fall of 1972. *Information*, October 1972, p. 1.

[18] Interview with Kenneth Gibson by the writer, November 2, 1972.

[19] "Gibson Coalesces Discontented Groups in Newark--Immediacy Likely to be Focus of Planning," *Equalop: Quarterly Newsletter of Planners for Equal Opportunity,* 4 (Summer 1970), 4.

[20] Letter to the writer, November 12, 1973, from Philip LeB. Douglas, who as a Mayor's aide took an important part in handling the Ombudsman project during its early stages.

[21] Letter to the writer, October 3, 1973.

[22] Letter from Philip Douglas to the writer, November 12, 1973.

Notes to Chapter I cont'd

[23] Kenneth Gibson to Leonard S. Slaughter, Director of the Community Division, OEO, February 23, 1971.

[24] Letter from Stolfa to Jackson, September 15, 1971.

[25] Letter to the writer, November 12, 1973.

[26] For this curiously dangling clause, which was not removed from the ordinance, see the final version of the ordinance, Cl. 10(f), in Appendix II.

[27] Undated Stolfa memorandum to Stanley Anderson. He responded to some of her objections on December 7, 1971: (1) Why was OEO anxious to exempt courts? (2) Agreed that there should be a statement of qualifications. (3) Agreed that the Ombudsman's term should be longer than the Mayor's. (4) Agreed and thought it "crucial" that the Ombudsman should be removed only for disability or malfeasance. (5) Agreed that Cl. 9(e) was unnecessary but advised that since it did no harm, "I should give it a low priority in terms of the changes which you try to accomplish in this Ordinance." (6) Stolfa's sixth point not mentioned by Anderson. (7) Agreed that an immunity provision was "important." (8) Conflict of interest provision not mentioned by Anderson. Whether because of Anderson's influence or for some other reason, the first and fifth changes suggested by Stolfa in her memorandum were not made in the ordinance. The same day he responded to the Stolfa memorandum, Anderson wrote to Ira Jackson stating his opinion that the draft ordinance was "weak in establishing the independence of the Ombudsman," particularly in allowing the Mayor to remove him at his discretion. "Surely," he urged, "there must be some way that removal can be conditioned upon cause--such as 'neglect of duty or misconduct,' to use the language of the Gellhorn statute."

Notes to Chapter I cont'd

[28] By this time, Ira Jackson and Philip Douglas
had left the Mayor's office and Norman Abrams, another
young Brandeis and Harvard graduate who recently become an assistant to the Mayor, assumed main responsibility for the Ombudsman policy. Another aide much involved during this period was Marvin McGraw, a young
native of Newark who has largely given up the role of
Black militant he filled as a political science student at the Newark branch of Rutgers, to enact a more
moderate one within the Gibson administration. Abrams,
who has abandoned a scholarly career as an urban his-
torian because he feels the need actively to try to do
something about Newark's plight, fits within a recent
description of the Mayor's personal staff as tending
"to be predominantly composed of young, devoted, in-
telligent but inexperienced white aides, whom the May-
or described as the best staff available for the money."
Fred Barbaro, "Newark: Political Brokers," *Society*,
9 (September-October, 1972), p. 54.

[29] Anderson to Norman Abrams, January 20, 1972.
Anderson did suggest one small clarification in the
ordinance, which was accepted.


## NOTES TO CHAPTER II

[1] In 1970, the eligible electorate was almost
evenly divided: 47% white and 45% Black. Thomas R.
Brooks, "Breakdown in Newark," *Dissent* (Winter 1972),
p. 135.

[2] *Interim Report of the Task Force on Urban Programs*, November 9, 1971.

[3] This account of positions taken during the council meeting is based on the report in the New York

# Notes to Chapter II cont'd

*Times* of January 7th and on the Council Minutes for January 5, 1972, pp. 23-26.

[4] For a full account of these matters, see Philip LeB. Douglas, "Reform in Newark: The Response to Crisis, 1953-1972." A senior thesis presented to the Faculty of the Woodrow Wilson School of Public and International Affairs, Princeton University, April 14, 1972.

[5] See "Newark's Plight in Perspective," *Urban Consensus* (April 1972), n.p.

[6] Councilman-at-Large Earl Harris and Councilman Sharpe James of the South Ward. The Rev. Dennis A. Westbrooks appears to have an approach to his constituents different from that of his two Black colleagues. Representing the predominantly Black Central Ward, he is more racially militant and ideological than James and Harris. Also, not having come to Newark until 1967, he has not been reared in the Newark political system, unlike Harris, who was brought to Newark as a baby in 1923, or James, who was born there. Westbrooks seems to be very popular among the inhabitants of the Central Ward because of his reputation as a successful and vigorous defender of their collective interests.

[7] A self-made man, Gibson in 1962 obtained a degree from the Newark College of Engineering to become one of the few Black professional engineers in New Jersey. While at night school he had worked for the New Jersey Highway Department; after qualifying as an engineer at thirty, he moved to the Newark Housing Authority. Thus, although having no experience of elective office until he was 38, Gibson when elected Mayor had had several years' personal experience of Newark governmental administration and its corruption and inefficiency.

## Notes to Chapter II cont'd

[8] The New York *Times*, September 20, 1970, pp. 1, 68. Gibson has commented, "I'm an engineer, as you know, by personality, too, and I try to rule out things that are done for dramatic or public relations value." An interview in the New York *Post*, July 4, 1970, as quoted in *Current Biography Yearbook, 1971*, p. 152.

[9] Although this ideal typical analysis helps in understanding the actions of a politician such as Kenneth Gibson, no actual person, including Gibson, completely fits the description. Thus it should be noted that Gibson has made use of patronage to bolster his political position. However, unlike most other recent mayors of Newark, he has refused to use public positions requiring expertise as patronage. This partial deviation from the pure type may be one of the reasons he was re-elected in May 1974.

[10] Douglas, "Reform in Newark," pp. 191-195.

[11] The negotiations over the clerk's office must have taken place during a private meeting of the council on April 18th which the minutes for the 19th show was attended by Business Administrator Cornelius Bodine. Louis Turco and Anthony Giuliano were absent for the vote on the 19th, which went six to one for the Ombudsman resolution. This was the first of four occasions when Councilman Megaro voted against the Ombudsman.

[12] The minutes for the two council meetings suggest that Harris said little in favor of the Ombudsman. In October, he opposed the proposal. Administration bills are divided up among councilmen for introduction and seconding at their Tuesday private sessions.

[13] *Yes:* Bontempo, Bottone, Harris, James, Villani, and Westbrooks. *No:* Giuliano and Megaro. *Abstain:* Turco.

Notes to Chapter II cont'd

[14] Council Minutes for May 3, 1972, p. 9. Giuliano was president of the PBA both in 1965 and 1968 when the organization strongly opposed proposals for civilian review boards.

[15] The reasons for Megaro's persistent opposition remain obscure. A lawyer with an M.A. in Political Science and registered as a doctoral student in Political Science at the New School of Social Research, Megaro might have been expected to look favorably upon the Ombudsman idea. He was first elected to the council in 1970 (North Ward) and is the only councilman to be also a member of the New Jersey General Assembly, to which he was elected in November 1971. Significantly, when interviewed on August 2, 1973 by the writer's research assistant Lawrence Moore, Megaro immediately upon Moore's mentioning the word "Ombudsman" said that the Ombudsman was like a police review board.

[16] Bradley suggested that this information had come to the council from the Mayor's office, but he may have had in mind Harris, who seconded both readings of the ordinance. It seems extremely unlikely that if Harris was giving a signal on May 3rd for the possible later defeat of the Ombudsman, he was speaking for the Mayor's office. If he was speaking for anyone, it would have been the City Clerk's office.

[17] Washington has a B.A. degree from St. Peter's College, Jersey City, and went on to graduate *cum laude* (3rd in a class of 168) from Howard University Law School and to receive an LL.M. from Harvard Law School.

[18] The following account of the October 3rd meeting is based on a memorandum sent to the writer on October 9th by Norman Abrams, who was present.

Notes to Chapter II cont'd

[19] Kay was Acting Division Chief, Community Development Division, Office of Program Development, OEO.

[20] President Turco, who seconded the nomination, had also expressed concern about non-resident appointments but maintained that he was supporting Walker because he was so eminently qualified. Westbrooks, who introduced the nomination, and Bottone and Bontempo spoke in favor of the nomination, stressing Walker's ability and the need to fill the office. The vote was, *Yes:* Bontempo, Bottone, James, Villani, Westbrooks, Turco; *No:* Harris; *Abstain:* Giuliano and Megaro. Council Minutes, January 5, 1972, pp. 30-31.

[21] They were Bottone, Giuliano, Harris, James, Megaro. Newark *Star-Ledger,* October 12, 1972, p. 24.

[22] *Ibid.*

[23] *Ibid.*

[24] Interviewed by the writer on November 2, 1972. Ron Gasparinetti prides himself on being a tough cop. Joining the Newark police force in 1964, he soon aspired to heading the PBA. In April 1968, he joined with the 11 other members of the night motorcycle squad of the Traffic Division to form an "Aggressor Slate" to campaign for the 12 offices of the PBA to be filled that June. As the slate's candidate for PBA President, Gasparinetti announced, "We think we can work together for a unified, no-nonsense, get-tough policy." Newark *Evening News,* April 25, 1968, p. 9. Gasparinetti's efforts failed and he was obliged to wait four years until his ambition was fulfilled. As PBA President, he seems to have played a more aggressive role than his predecessor.

Notes to Chapter II cont'd

[25] Newark *Evening News*, May 8, 1968, p. 44.

[26] Newark *Star-Ledger*, October 16, 1972; Asbury Park *Press*, October 16, 1972; and Vailsburg *Leader*, October 19, 1972.

[27] Norman Abrams believes that the interview with Washington strongly contributed to the council's rejection of the office of Ombudsman. "Councilmen, I believe, did not realize it at first, but when they met Washington, they suddenly realized through the person the political potential of the office. They realized what a photogenic, capable, aggressive guy in the job could do to build up his own political position, maybe for a future run for Mayor or Council." Letter to the writer, December 8, 1973. However, in view of the fact that councilmanic opinion was running strongly against the Ombudsman by the end of September, it is difficult to see how the interview on October 17th could have had much effect on the success or failure of the project.

[28] The motion to return the resolution to the administration was made by Turco and seconded by Bontempo. Westbrooks was not present for the vote, and of the remaining two Black councilmen, Harris supported the motion and James opposed it.

[29] Bontempo, Giuliano, James, Turco. Silent Councilman Bottone also argued along this line when interviewed by the writer. Several councilmen either believed or professed to believe that the Ombudsman would be simply another referral agency such as Action Now. James took this position on October 18th and it was mentioned by Joseph Bradley, when interviewed, as one of the reasons the council had opposed the Ombudsman. According to Bradley, Robert Washington had weakened the case for the Ombudsman while being interviewed. When

Notes to Chapter II cont'd

asked what he would do after he received a complaint, Washington answered that he would first go to the department complained against. This answer led councilmen to conclude that Washington, himself, perceived the Ombudsman as a referral agency. Washington's reply can, of course, be interpreted differently.

[30] This position was articulated by Bontempo, Giuliano, and James.

[31] Giuliano, Harris, and James. Giuliano referred only to police protection as the needed service. According to Joseph Bradley, the council had recently decided that it would not receive just any money from the federal government but only that for basic city services.

[32] "Statement by Mayor Kenneth A. Gibson on returning of Ombudsman Federal Funds to Washington," October 19, 1972. The statement was reported in the Newark *Star-Ledger*, October 20, 1972, p. 33.

## NOTES TO CHAPTER III

[1] Westbrooks did not explain the votes of Bottone and Megaro.

[2] As a relic of past political corruption in the city, Ralph Villani also may not have looked kindly upon the Ombudsman, but, as we have seen in the case of Hugh Addonizio, support of political corruption and an Ombudsman are not necessarily incompatible. In 1949-53, Villani was the first Newark Mayor of Italian descent. A grand jury in the latter year found that he had participated in a systematic shakedown of city employees. Douglas, "Reform in Newark," pp. 25-27.

## Notes to Chapter III cont'd

[3] Letter to the writer, January 10, 1973.

[4] Letter from Philip Douglas to the writer, November 12, 1973.

[5] Anderson, *Ombudsmen for American Government?*, p. 146. Anderson observes that the Ombudsman has become a public issue in the United States only when it has been identified with a civilian police review board, in which case the clamor has been more against than for the office.

[6] Moore, *The Joint Seattle/King County Office of Citizen Complaints...*, pp. 5, I-8.

[7] Telephone interview of Edwin F. Melick by Lawrence Moore, August 2, 1973; Letter from Joel R. Jacobson to the writer, March 14, 1973.

[8] Telephone interview of Norman Abrams by the writer, July 6, 1973; Letter from Abrams to the writer, October 15, 1973.

[9] Interview of Patricia Stolfa by the writer, February 1, 1974.

[10] Moore, *...Seattle/King County Office...*, pp. 13-15. Councilman Liem Tuai of Seattle believes that use of the Citizens' Commission was helpful in overcoming objections to hiring a person from outside the state. See Stanley V. Anderson and John E. Moore (eds.), *Establishing Ombudsman Offices: Recent Experience in the United States* (Berkeley: Institute of Governmental Studies, University of California, 1972) pp. 47-48.

Notes to Chapter III cont'd

[11] Telephone interview with Abrams and McGraw, July 6, 1973.

[12] Letter from Douglas to the writer, November 12, 1973.

[13] For the distinction between classical and executive Ombudsmen, see Alan J. Wyner, ed., *Executive Ombudsmen in the United States* (Berkeley: Institute of Governmental Studies, University of California, 1973) pp. 10-13, 305-315.

## ACTION NOW STATISTICS
## FISCAL YEAR 1971-1972

|  | Processed | Completed | Pending |
|---|---|---|---|
| Abandoned Cars | 87 | 62 | 25 |
| Animals | 101 | 76 | 25 |
| Aged | 2 | 2 | 0 |
| Air Pollution | 10 | 6 | 4 |
| Business Loans | 13 | 10 | 3 |
| Consumer Protection | 112 | 88 | 24 |
| Day Care | 2 | 2 | 0 |
| Human Rights | 70 | 57 | 12 |
| Education | 42 | 37 | 5 |
| Employment | 98 | 94 | 4 |
| Family Counseling | 14 | 13 | 1 |
| Health | 199 | 155 | 44 |
| Housing | 1,728 | 1,203 | 525 |
| Information and Misc. | 80,206 | 80,190 | 16 |
| Legal | 246 | 188 | 58 |
| Licenses | 2 | 2 | 0 |
| Medicaid | 17 | 17 | 0 |
| Mental Health | 1 | 1 | 0 |
| Narcotics-Alcoholism | 15 | 15 | 0 |
| Police | 547 | 431 | 111 |
| Political Information | 10 | 10 | 0 |
| Recreation | 1 | 1 | 0 |
| Sanitation-Public Works | 632 | 479 | 153 |
| Social Security | 13 | 12 | 1 |
| Taxes & Insurance | 9 | 9 | 0 |
| Traffic | 25 | 10 | 15 |
| Utilities | 61 | 52 | 9 |
| Veterans | 12 | 12 | 0 |
| Unwed Mothers | 173 | 170 | 3 |
| Welfare | 291 | 249 | 42 |
| Salvation Army | 14 | 14 | 0 |
| Rat & Pest | 67 | 34 | 33 |
| Public Works | 113 | 81 | 32 |

|  | Processed | Completed | Pending |
|---|---|---|---|
| Inspections | 1,323 | 924 | 399 |
| Parks & Grounds | 77 | 23 | 54 |
| Demolition | 30 | 5 | 25 |
| Water Department | 4 | 0 | 4 |
| Fire Department | 61 | 37 | 24 |
| Essex County | 16 | 9 | 7 |
| Miscellaneous | 61 | 56 | 5 |
| TOTALS | 87,000 | 85,267 | 1,733 |

Note: From the *First Annual Report of Action Now*, p. 20.

# APPENDIX II

## TEXT OF THE NEWARK OMBUDSMAN ORDINANCE

AN ORDINANCE PROVIDING FOR THE
APPOINTMENT, TERM OF OFFICE, DUTIES
AND QUALIFICATIONS OF AN OMBUDSMAN
FOR THE CITY OF NEWARK, NEW JERSEY
AND PROVIDING FOR AN EXECUTIVE STAFF
AND SUPPORT STAFF WITHIN THAT OFFICE.

BE IT ORDAINED BY THE MUNICIPAL COUNCIL OF THE CITY OF NEWARK, NEW JERSEY, THAT:

1. *Definitions.* As used in this Ordinance, of

(a) "Administrative Agency" means any department or other governmental unit, any official, or any employee of the City of Newark, except that the Mayor, Deputy Mayor (2), Mayoral Administrative Aides (4), Municipal Council, field Representatives of the Council (9), The Office of the City Clerk, the Clerk to the Municipal Council, and all employees of the Office of City Clerk, shall not be included.

(b) "Administrative Act" includes every action (such as decisions, omissions, recommendations, practices, or procedures) of an administrative agency.

2. *Establishment of Office of Ombudsman.* The Office of the Ombudsman is hereby established as an independent agency of the City of Newark.

3. *Appointment and Term of Office.* The Mayor shall appoint the Ombudsman subject to the advice and consent of the Municipal Council of the City of Newark.

4. *Qualifications.* The Ombudsman shall be a person well equipped to analyze problems of law, administration, and public policy, and shall not be actively involved in partisan affairs.

87

5. *Term of Office.*

(a)  The Ombudsman shall serve for a term of five years, unless removed by recommendation of the Mayor and a vote of two-thirds of the members of the Municipal Council, upon their determining that he has become incapacitated or has been guilty of neglect of duty or misconduct.

(b)  The five year term of office of the Ombudsman shall in no way obligate the City of Newark to finance the Office of Ombudsman beyond the two year budget to be paid for by the Office of Economic Opportunity.

6.  *Salary.*  The Ombudsman shall receive a salary of $30,000 per year. During his term of office, he shall devote full time to the job. He shall not hold or be a candidate for any other public office; and he shall not be engaged in any other occupation for reward or profit.

7.  *Executive Staff.*  The Ombudsman shall have the power (within the amounts available by appropriation) to hire an executive staff, sufficient in number and qualifications as he may deem necessary to fulfill his duties. The executive staff shall serve a term co-terminus with that of the Ombudsman, unless earlier discharged by him.

8.  *Deputy Ombudsman.*  The Ombudsman shall designate one of his assistants to be the Deputy Ombudsman, with the authority to act in his stead and fulfill the duties of his office when he himself is disabled or protractedly absent. If the Office of Ombudsman becomes vacant for any cause, the Deputy Ombudsman shall serve as Acting Ombudsman until an Ombudsman has been appointed for a full term.

9.  *Support Staff.*  The Ombudsman may (within the amounts available by appropriation) hire a support staff of clerical personnel sufficient in number and qualification as he may deem necessary to fulfill his

duties. These employees shall enjoy Civil Service status.

10. *Powers*. The Ombudsman shall have the following powers:

(a) He may investigate, on complaint or on his own motion, any administrative act of any administrative agency;

(b) He may prescribe the methods of which complaints are to be made, received, and acted upon, he may determine the scope and manner of investigations to be made; and, subject to the requirements of this Act, he may determine the form, frequency, and distribution of his conclusions and recommendations;

(c) He may request and shall be given by each administrative agency the assistance and information he deems necessary for the discharge of his responsibilities; he may examine the records and documents of all administrative agencies; and he may enter and inspect premises within any administrative agency's control;

(d) He may administer oaths and hold hearings in connection with any matter under inquiry;

(e) He may undertake, participate in, or cooperate with general studies or inquiries, whether or not related to any particular administrative agency or any particular administrative act, if he believes that they may enhance knowledge about or lead to improvements in the functioning of administrative agencies;

(f) He shall refer all other complaints to an appropriate public or private agency.

11. *Delegation*. The Ombudsman, or the Deputy Ombudsman, either in his capacity as Acting Ombudsman or on account of the disability or protracted absence of the Ombudsman, as provided in section 8 hereof, may

delegate to members of his staff any of his authorities or duties under this law, except this power of delegation and the duty of formally making recommendations to agencies or reports to the Mayor or the Municipal Council.

12. *Matters Appropriate for Investigation.* In selecting matters for his attention, the Ombudsman should address himself particularly to an administrative act that might be:

(a)  contrary to law or regulation;

(b)  unreasonable, unfair, or inconsistent with the general course of an administrative agency's functioning;

(c)  mistaken in law or arbitrary in ascertainments of facts;

(d)  improper in motivation or based on irrelevant considerations;

(e)  unclear or inadequately explained when reasons should have been revealed;

(f)  inefficiently performed; or

(g)  otherwise objectionable.

13. *Action on Complaints.*

(a)  The Ombudsman may receive a complaint from any source concerning an administrative act. He shall conduct a suitable investigation into things complained of unless he believes that:

(1)  the complainant has available to him another administrative remedy or channel of complaint which he could reasonably be expected to use;

(2) the grievance pertains to a matter outside the Ombudsman's power;

(3) the complainant's interest is insufficiently related to the subject matter;

(4) the complaint is trivial, frivolous, vexatious, or not made in good faith;

(5) other complaints are more worthy of attention;

(6) The Ombudsman's resources are insufficient for adequate investigations; or

(7) the complaint has been too long delayed to justify present examination of its merit.

(b) After completing his consideration of a complaint (whether or not it has been investigated) the Ombudsman shall suitably inform the complainant and the administrative agency or agencies involved.

(c) The Ombudsman's declining to investigate a complaint shall not, however, bar him from proceeding on his own motion to inquire into the matter complained about or into related problems.

14. *Consultation With Agency.* Before announcing a conclusion or recommendation that criticizes an administrative agency or any person, the Ombudsman shall consult with that agency or person.

15. *Recommendations.*

(a) If, having considered a complaint and whatever material he deems pertinent, the Ombudsman is of the opinion that an administrative agency should (1) consider the matter further, (2) modify or cancel an administrative act, (3) alter a regulation or ruling, (4) explain more fully the administrative act in question, or (5) take any other step, he shall state his recommendations to the administrative agency. If the Ombudsman so requests, the agency shall, within the time he has specified, inform him about the action taken on his recommendations or the reasons for not complying with them.

16. *Publications of Recommendations.* The Ombudsman may publish his conclusions, recommendations, and suggestions by transmitting them to the Mayor, the Municipal Council or any of its committees, the press, and others who may be concerned. When publishing an opinion adverse to an administrative agency or official he shall (unless excused by the agency or official affected) include the substance of any statement the administrative agency or official may have made to him by way of explaining past difficulties or present rejection of the Ombudsman's proposals.

17. *Reports.* In addition to whatever reports he may make from time to time, the Ombudsman shall on or about February 15th of each year report to the Municipal Council and to the Mayor concerning the exercise of his functions during the preceding calendar year. In discussing matters with which he has dealt, the Ombudsman need not identify those immediately concerned if to do so would cause needless hardship. So far as the annual report may criticize named agencies or officials, it must also include the substance of their replies to the criticism.

18. *Disciplinary Action Against Public Personnel.* If the Ombudsman has reason to believe that any public (official) employee, or other person has acted in a manner warranting criminal or disciplinary proceedings, he shall refer the matter to the appropriate authorities.

19. *Savings Clause.* If any provision of this ordinance, or its application to any person or circumstance is held invalid, the remainder of the ordinance,

or the application of the provision to other persons or circumstances, is not affected.

20. *Effective Date.* This act shall take effect immediately.

INSTITUTE OF GOVERNMENTAL STUDIES
109 Moses Hall, University of California
Berkeley, California 94720

## OMBUDSMAN RESEARCH

### MONOGRAPHS

Alan J. Wyner
*The Nebraska Ombudsman: Innovation in State Government.* 160pp
1974   $6.75

Mikael Hidén
*The Ombudsman in Finland: The First Fifty Years.* 198pp   1973   $8.00

Kent M. Weeks
*Ombudsmen Around the World: A Comparative Chart.* 101pp   1973
$3.00

Alan J. Wyner, ed.
*Executive Ombudsmen in the United States.* 315pp   1973   $5.50

Timothy L. Fitzharris
*The Desirability of a Correctional Ombudsman.* 114pp   1973   $3.00

Stanley V. Anderson and John E. Moore, eds.
*Establishing Ombudsman Offices: Recent Experience in the United States.*
293pp   1972   $3.00

Lance Tibbles and John H. Hollands
*Buffalo Citizens Administrative Service: An Ombudsman Demonstration
Project.* 90pp   1970   $2.75

Stanley V. Anderson
*Ombudsman Papers: American Experience and Proposals.* 407pp   1969
$3.75

Stanley Scott, ed.
*Western American Assembly on the Ombudsman: Report.* 36pp   1968
$1.00

Dean Mann
*The Citizen and the Bureaucracy: Complaint-Handling Procedures of Three
California Legislators.* 52pp   1968   $1.25

Stanley V. Anderson
*Canadian Ombudsman Proposals.* 168pp   1966   $2.50

California residents add 6 percent sales tax; residents of Alameda, Contra Costa and
San Francisco counties add 6½ percent sales tax. Prepay orders under $10.00.

PUBLIC AFFAIRS REPORTS

Alan J. Wyner
"Lieutenant Governors as Political Ombudsmen." v. 12, no. 6, 1971
Carl E. Schwarz
"The Mexican Writ of Amparo: An Extraordinary Remedy Against Official Abuse of Individual Rights: Part I." v. 10, no. 6, 1969; and Part II, v. 11, no. 1, 1970.
Stanley V. Anderson
"Ombudsman Proposals: Stimulus to Inquiry." v. 7, no. 6, 1966    4pp

"The Ombudsman: Public Defender Against Maladministration." v. 6, no. 2, 1965    4pp


*Public Affairs Reports* are now available in collected volumes; *Emerging Issues in Public Policy: Research Reports and Essays.* The 1960–1965 volume and the 1966–1972 volume are $11.00 each.


REPRINTS

John E. Moore
"Ombudsman and the Ghetto," 1 *Connecticut Law Review* (2)    December 1968  (IGS   Reprint   #39)
Lance Tibbles
"Ombudsmen for American Prisons," 48 *North Dakota Law Review* (3) Spring 1972   (IGS   Reprint   #44)